TROJAN EXPOSED

CYBER DEFENSE AND SECURITY PROTOCOLS FOR MALWARE ERADICATION

4 BOOKS IN 1

BOOK 1
TROJAN EXPOSED: A BEGINNER'S GUIDE TO CYBERSECURITY

BOOK 2
TROJAN EXPOSED: MASTERING ADVANCED THREAT DETECTION

BOOK 3
TROJAN EXPOSED: EXPERT STRATEGIES FOR CYBER RESILIENCE

BOOK 4
TROJAN EXPOSED: RED TEAM TACTICS AND ETHICAL HACKING

ROB BOTWRIGHT

Published by Rob Botwright
Library of Congress Cataloging-in-Publication Data
ISBN 978-1-83938-659-6
Cover design by Rizzo

Disclaimer

The contents of this book are based on extensive research and the best available historical sources. However, the author and publisher make no claims, promises, or guarantees about the accuracy, completeness, or adequacy of the information contained herein. The information in this book is provided on an "as is" basis, and the author and publisher disclaim any and all liability for any errors, omissions, or inaccuracies in the information or for any actions taken in reliance on such information. The opinions and views expressed in this book are those of the author and do not necessarily reflect the official policy or position of any organization or individual mentioned in this book. Any reference to specific people, places, or events is intended only to provide historical context and is not intended to defame or malign any group, individual, or entity. The information in this book is intended for educational and entertainment purposes only. It is not intended to be a substitute for professional advice or judgment. Readers are encouraged to conduct their own research and to seek professional advice where appropriate. Every effort has been made to obtain necessary permissions and acknowledgments for all images and other copyrighted material used in this book. Any errors or omissions in this regard are unintentional, and the author and publisher will correct them in future editions.

Introduction

Welcome to "Trojan Exposed: Cyber Defense and Security Protocols for Malware Eradication," a comprehensive book bundle that delves into the intricate world of cybersecurity, with a specific focus on combating one of the most notorious threats – the Trojan horse. This bundle consists of four meticulously crafted books, each designed to equip you with the knowledge, skills, and strategies necessary to protect your digital assets and navigate the evolving landscape of cyber threats.

In an era defined by the relentless growth of technology and connectivity, the digital realm is both a playground for innovation and a battleground for cyber warfare. Malicious actors constantly seek to exploit vulnerabilities, infiltrate systems, and compromise data. Among the arsenal of cyber threats, the Trojan horse stands as a symbol of deception and covert infiltration, capable of wreaking havoc on individuals, organizations, and nations.

This book bundle is your guide through the multifaceted world of Trojan malware and cybersecurity. Whether you are a novice seeking to grasp the fundamentals of cybersecurity or a seasoned professional looking to master advanced threat detection, this collection has something to offer. Together, these books provide a comprehensive roadmap for building a robust cybersecurity defense, preparing for cyber resilience, and even understanding the tactics of ethical hackers who work to protect against malicious attacks.

Let's take a closer look at each book within this bundle:
Book 1: "Trojan Exposed: A Beginner's Guide to Cybersecurity" serves as an introductory voyage into the realm of cybersecurity. Here, we provide foundational knowledge and essential principles that are vital for anyone seeking to understand the cyber threat landscape. We demystify cybersecurity concepts, explain the

history of Trojans, and offer actionable insights for safeguarding digital environments.

Book 2: "Trojan Exposed: Mastering Advanced Threat Detection" takes a deep dive into the intricacies of Trojan variants and advanced detection techniques. With a focus on identifying and mitigating sophisticated threats, this book equips you with the expertise needed to protect against evolving Trojan attacks.

Book 3: "Trojan Exposed: Expert Strategies for Cyber Resilience" shifts the focus to resilience and preparedness. It offers expert strategies for building cyber resilience, ensuring that your systems can withstand and recover from cyberattacks. By implementing these strategies, you will be better prepared to face the ever-changing threat landscape.

Book 4: "Trojan Exposed: Red Team Tactics and Ethical Hacking" takes an offensive approach to cybersecurity. We explore the techniques employed by ethical hackers and red teamers to simulate real-world cyberattacks. By understanding these tactics, you can better protect your systems, identify vulnerabilities, and enhance your overall cybersecurity posture.

As you embark on this journey through "Trojan Exposed," remember that cybersecurity is not merely a technological challenge; it's a dynamic field that demands continuous learning and adaptation. By the end of this book bundle, you will be well-prepared to defend against Trojan threats and navigate the complex world of cybersecurity with confidence.

Join us in this exploration of cybersecurity, as we uncover the inner workings of Trojans, develop advanced threat detection capabilities, build cyber resilience, and even explore the tactics of ethical hackers. Together, we will fortify our defenses and work towards a safer digital future.

BOOK 1
TROJAN EXPOSED
A BEGINNER'S GUIDE TO CYBERSECURITY

ROB BOTWRIGHT

Chapter 1: Understanding the Cyber Threat Landscape

In the world of cybersecurity, understanding cyber threats and their impact is fundamental. Cyber threats encompass a wide range of malicious activities and tactics that can disrupt, compromise, or damage computer systems, networks, and digital assets. These threats have evolved significantly over the years, becoming more sophisticated and persistent, posing a constant challenge to organizations and individuals alike.

One of the most common and widely recognized cyber threats is malware. Malware, short for malicious software, is a broad category that includes viruses, worms, Trojans, ransomware, spyware, and more. Each type of malware has its own specific method of infection and objectives, making them versatile tools for cybercriminals. Malware can infect devices and systems, steal sensitive data, disrupt operations, or even take control of compromised computers.

Another prevalent cyber threat is phishing, a form of social engineering. Phishing attacks involve the use of deceptive emails, websites, or messages that impersonate trusted entities to trick recipients into divulging confidential information such as passwords, credit card numbers, or login credentials. These attacks often appear genuine and exploit human psychology, making them a favored tactic among cybercriminals.

Beyond malware and phishing, there are distributed denial of service (DDoS) attacks, which flood target websites or servers with overwhelming traffic, rendering them inaccessible to legitimate users. These attacks can disrupt online services, cause financial losses, and damage an organization's reputation.

Additionally, there are advanced persistent threats (APTs), which are long-term, targeted attacks typically orchestrated by state-sponsored actors or organized cybercriminal groups. APTs are highly sophisticated and often involve multiple stages of infiltration, including reconnaissance, initial access, privilege escalation, and data exfiltration.

Ransomware, another insidious threat, has gained notoriety for encrypting victims' data and demanding a ransom for its release. Ransomware attacks can cripple businesses, healthcare institutions, and critical infrastructure, leading to significant financial and operational damage.

In recent years, supply chain attacks have emerged as a growing concern. These attacks exploit vulnerabilities in software supply chains, compromising trusted software vendors to distribute malicious code to unsuspecting users. Supply chain attacks can have far-reaching consequences, affecting numerous organizations and users who rely on compromised software.

The impact of cyber threats can be devastating. Financial losses from cyberattacks can reach billions of dollars, and the cost of recovery can be equally high. Beyond financial implications, cyberattacks can erode trust and damage the reputation of businesses and institutions. Data breaches can lead to the exposure of sensitive information, including personal, financial, and healthcare records, causing significant harm to individuals affected.

To combat cyber threats effectively, organizations and individuals must adopt proactive cybersecurity measures. This includes implementing robust security policies, regularly updating software and systems, educating employees and users about safe online practices, and deploying security technologies such as firewalls, antivirus software, intrusion detection systems (IDS), and intrusion prevention systems (IPS).

Furthermore, staying informed about the latest threats and vulnerabilities is crucial. Cybersecurity professionals and enthusiasts often rely on various sources, including threat intelligence feeds, security blogs, and forums, to stay updated on emerging threats and attack techniques. These sources provide valuable insights into evolving cyber threats and offer recommendations for mitigating risks.

In the realm of cybersecurity, the command line interface (CLI) plays a vital role in managing and securing systems. For example, administrators often use CLI commands to configure firewalls, set up access controls, and monitor network traffic. Additionally, they can employ command-line tools to scan for vulnerabilities, conduct penetration testing, and analyze system logs for signs of suspicious activity.

Deploying robust security measures is not only the responsibility of organizations but also individuals. Personal cybersecurity hygiene is crucial for protecting sensitive data and online accounts. Individuals can enhance their security by using strong, unique passwords for each account, enabling multi-factor authentication (MFA) wherever possible, and being cautious of unsolicited messages and emails.

In summary, cyber threats pose a constant and evolving risk in the digital age, impacting individuals, businesses, and critical infrastructure. These threats range from malware and phishing to DDoS attacks, APTs, and supply chain compromises. The consequences of cyberattacks can be severe, encompassing financial losses, data breaches, and reputational damage. To defend against these threats, proactive cybersecurity measures, education, and vigilance are essential. The CLI serves as a valuable tool for managing and securing systems, and staying informed about the latest threats and vulnerabilities is crucial for effective defense.

Historical perspectives on cybersecurity offer valuable insights into the evolution of digital security measures and the challenges that have shaped the field over time.

In the early days of computing, security concerns were relatively minimal, as computers were large and isolated, with limited connectivity.

The primary focus was on physical security to protect mainframe computers and their data centers from unauthorized access.

As computers became more accessible and interconnected, the need for stronger security measures became evident.

In the 1970s and 1980s, with the advent of personal computers and the growth of the internet, cybersecurity challenges escalated.

The first notable computer virus, the "Creeper," emerged in the early 1970s, highlighting the vulnerability of interconnected systems.

To counteract this growing threat, the concept of antivirus software was introduced, aimed at identifying and removing malicious software from computer systems.

The 1980s saw the proliferation of malware, including the infamous "Morris Worm" in 1988, which caused significant disruptions across the early internet.

To address these threats, organizations and individuals began to adopt firewalls, a critical component of network security, to control incoming and outgoing network traffic.

However, the cybersecurity landscape continued to evolve rapidly, with hackers and cybercriminals becoming more sophisticated in their techniques.

The 1990s brought the rise of e-commerce and online banking, introducing new opportunities for cybercriminals to exploit vulnerabilities and steal sensitive financial information.

In response, encryption technologies like SSL (Secure Sockets Layer) and its successor, TLS (Transport Layer Security), were developed to secure online transactions and protect data in transit.

The late 1990s also witnessed the emergence of intrusion detection systems (IDS) and intrusion prevention systems (IPS), which helped organizations detect and respond to network-based threats.

The early 2000s saw the proliferation of phishing attacks, where cybercriminals used deceptive emails and websites to trick individuals into revealing personal and financial information.

This led to the adoption of email filtering and spam detection technologies to reduce the impact of phishing attempts.

In 2003, the world witnessed the "SQL Slammer" worm, which infected hundreds of thousands of computers within minutes of its release, underscoring the importance of timely software patching and vulnerability management.

Around the same time, the U.S. government introduced the Federal Information Security Management Act (FISMA) to improve cybersecurity practices across federal agencies.

The mid-2000s marked the rise of botnets, networks of compromised computers controlled by cybercriminals to carry out various malicious activities, including distributed denial of service (DDoS) attacks and spam campaigns.

Security professionals responded by developing better botnet detection and mitigation techniques.

In 2008, the introduction of the Conficker worm demonstrated the persistence of cybersecurity challenges, as it infected millions of computers worldwide and exploited unpatched vulnerabilities.

This incident highlighted the need for proactive and comprehensive cybersecurity measures.

The increasing reliance on mobile devices and the proliferation of mobile applications in the late 2000s brought forth new security concerns, as mobile platforms became targets for malware and data breaches.

Mobile device management (MDM) solutions and mobile security best practices became essential for protecting smartphones and tablets.

The 2010s saw a surge in data breaches, with high-profile incidents affecting major corporations, government agencies, and social media platforms.

This prompted the introduction of data breach notification laws and heightened awareness of the importance of data protection.

Cybersecurity frameworks and standards, such as NIST Cybersecurity Framework and GDPR (General Data Protection Regulation), emerged to guide organizations in improving their security posture and compliance.

Throughout this period, the role of ethical hacking, or penetration testing, gained prominence, as organizations recognized the value of employing skilled professionals to identify and address vulnerabilities before malicious actors could exploit them.

Cybersecurity education and certification programs, such as Certified Ethical Hacker (CEH) and Certified Information Systems Security Professional (CISSP), became essential for building a competent workforce.

As the 2020s began, the COVID-19 pandemic accelerated the shift to remote work, introducing new cybersecurity challenges related to securing remote access, virtual private networks (VPNs), and collaboration tools.

The SolarWinds breach in late 2020 highlighted the sophisticated nature of supply chain attacks and underscored the importance of robust supply chain security practices.

Looking ahead, the future of cybersecurity will likely involve advancements in artificial intelligence (AI) and machine learning (ML) for threat detection, as well as the continued development of quantum-resistant encryption to protect against emerging quantum computing threats.

Ultimately, the history of cybersecurity serves as a testament to the ongoing battle between defenders and attackers in the digital realm, emphasizing the need for vigilance, adaptability, and a commitment to staying one step ahead of evolving threats.

Chapter 2: Introduction to Trojans and Malware

Malware, short for malicious software, is a ubiquitous and ever-evolving category of digital threats that continues to pose significant risks to computer systems, networks, and the data they store. Understanding what malware is and how it operates is crucial for anyone navigating the digital landscape.

At its core, malware is any software intentionally designed to cause harm, steal data, or gain unauthorized access to computer systems or networks. It encompasses a wide range of malicious programs, each with its own specific functionality and objectives.

One of the most common forms of malware is the computer virus. Viruses are self-replicating programs that attach themselves to legitimate files or programs, allowing them to spread to other files and systems when the infected files are executed. This replication mechanism is akin to the way biological viruses propagate within living organisms.

Another prevalent type of malware is the worm. Worms are self-contained programs that do not require a host file for propagation. Instead, they exploit vulnerabilities in software or network protocols to spread from one system to another. Worms can rapidly infect a large number of computers and disrupt networks by overloading them with traffic.

Trojans, short for Trojan horses, are deceptive malware that disguise themselves as legitimate software or files to trick users into executing them. Once executed, Trojans typically perform unauthorized actions, such as stealing sensitive data, granting remote access to the attacker, or opening a backdoor for future attacks.

Ransomware has gained notoriety in recent years due to its destructive impact. Ransomware encrypts a victim's files or entire system, rendering them inaccessible. The attacker then demands a ransom in exchange for the decryption key, effectively holding the victim's data hostage until payment is made.

Spyware is a stealthy form of malware designed to spy on users and collect information without their knowledge or consent. It can monitor keystrokes, capture screenshots, record web browsing habits, and harvest personal data, including login credentials and financial information.

Adware, on the other hand, is a type of malware that displays unwanted advertisements to users. While adware may not be as harmful as other malware types, it can be extremely annoying and negatively impact a user's browsing experience.

Botnets are networks of compromised computers, or "bots," controlled by a central command-and-control server. Cybercriminals use botnets to carry out various malicious activities, such as launching distributed denial of service (DDoS) attacks, sending spam emails, or conducting coordinated attacks on websites.

Understanding how malware operates requires a deeper look into its lifecycle. The lifecycle of malware typically consists of several stages, including infection, execution, propagation, and payload delivery.

In the infection stage, malware gains access to a target system. This can occur through various means, such as exploiting software vulnerabilities, tricking users into downloading malicious files, or leveraging social engineering tactics in phishing emails.

Once on a system, the malware executes its code. This may involve modifying system files, adding registry entries, or creating new processes to maintain persistence. Some malware is designed to evade detection by employing rootkit techniques that hide their presence from security software.

Propagation is a critical phase for many types of malware, especially worms and viruses. Malware seeks to spread to other systems or devices to maximize its impact. This can occur through network vulnerabilities, email attachments, or infected files shared among users.

Payload delivery is the ultimate objective of most malware. The payload can vary widely depending on the malware's purpose. It may involve stealing sensitive data, encrypting files, granting remote access to the attacker, or initiating other malicious actions.

To combat malware effectively, individuals and organizations must implement comprehensive cybersecurity measures. This includes keeping software and operating systems up to date with the latest security patches to minimize vulnerabilities that malware can exploit.

Deploying robust antivirus and anti-malware solutions is essential for real-time threat detection and removal. These security tools use signature-based and heuristic analysis to identify and quarantine or remove known and suspicious malware.

Firewalls play a vital role in network security by monitoring incoming and outgoing traffic and blocking potentially malicious connections. Network segmentation can isolate critical systems and data from potential threats.

User education is also crucial in preventing malware infections. Teaching individuals how to recognize phishing emails, avoid suspicious downloads, and practice good cybersecurity hygiene can significantly reduce the risk of malware infections.

For system administrators, monitoring and logging network traffic and system events can help detect malware activity early. Security information and event management (SIEM) solutions can assist in identifying anomalous behavior and potential breaches.

Regular backups of critical data are essential to mitigate the impact of ransomware attacks. Ensuring that backups are offline or isolated from the network prevents them from being encrypted or compromised in the event of an attack.

While malware continues to evolve and adapt, cybersecurity professionals and researchers work tirelessly to develop new detection and prevention techniques. Behavioral analysis, machine learning, and threat intelligence are valuable tools in staying ahead of emerging threats.

In summary, malware represents a broad and ever-present threat in the digital landscape. It encompasses various types, each with its own malicious objectives. Understanding how malware operates and implementing robust cybersecurity measures is essential for protecting systems, data, and users from its harmful effects.

In the realm of malicious software, commonly referred to as malware, Trojans hold a distinctive and insidious position.

Named after the legendary wooden horse of ancient Greek mythology, these malicious programs masquerade as benign or useful software while concealing their true destructive or harmful intentions.

The deceptive nature of Trojans makes them a potent tool for cybercriminals, as they trick users into willingly installing or executing the malware.

Unlike viruses and worms, which self-replicate and spread independently, Trojans rely on human interaction to propagate, often through social engineering tactics or by exploiting software vulnerabilities.

Trojans can take on various forms and functions, making them versatile tools for cybercriminals and hackers.

Some Trojans are designed to steal sensitive data, such as login credentials, credit card numbers, or personal information, by logging keystrokes or capturing screenshots.

Others may create backdoors on infected systems, allowing attackers to gain unauthorized access, control compromised computers remotely, or use them as part of a botnet.

Furthermore, Trojans can be used to deliver additional malware payloads, facilitating the installation of other malicious software on the victim's system.

The primary objective of Trojans often dictates their classification into different categories, each tailored to a specific malicious purpose.

One common category of Trojans is banking Trojans, which are specifically crafted to steal financial information.

These Trojans often target online banking users, intercepting login credentials, hijacking banking sessions, and redirecting funds to the attacker's accounts.

Another category is remote access Trojans (RATs), which provide attackers with complete control over compromised systems.

Attackers can use RATs to perform a wide range of malicious activities, including data theft, surveillance, and launching additional attacks from the compromised system.

Keyloggers are a subset of Trojans that focus on recording a user's keystrokes.

They can capture sensitive information such as passwords, credit card numbers, and other typed data, which attackers can then exploit for financial gain or unauthorized access.

Trojan downloaders and droppers are designed to deliver other malware payloads to the victim's system.

Once executed, they initiate the download and installation of additional malicious software, expanding the attacker's control and capabilities on the compromised system.

An interesting aspect of Trojans is their ability to adapt and evolve over time.

As security measures and technologies advance, cybercriminals continually develop new techniques and tactics to bypass defenses and increase the effectiveness of Trojans.

To combat Trojans effectively, individuals and organizations must adopt a multi-layered cybersecurity approach.

This includes implementing security software that includes antivirus, anti-malware, and intrusion detection capabilities to detect and quarantine Trojan infections.

Regular software updates and patch management are crucial to address vulnerabilities that Trojans often exploit.

Maintaining up-to-date security patches helps reduce the attack surface and minimizes the risk of successful Trojan infections.

Firewalls and network monitoring tools play a vital role in identifying and blocking suspicious network traffic associated with Trojan activity.

Network segmentation can also limit the spread of Trojans within an organization's network.

User education is equally important in preventing Trojan infections.

Training individuals to recognize phishing emails, avoid downloading attachments or clicking on suspicious links, and practicing safe online habits can help reduce the likelihood of falling victim to Trojan attacks.

For system administrators and security professionals, monitoring network traffic and system logs can help detect and respond to Trojan activity promptly.

Security information and event management (SIEM) solutions can aid in identifying anomalous behavior and potential Trojan infections.

In some cases, manual removal of Trojans may be necessary.

This involves using command-line interface (CLI) commands or specialized removal tools to identify and eliminate the Trojan from the infected system.

However, manual removal can be complex and risky, as it requires a deep understanding of the specific Trojan's behavior and system impact.

For this reason, many security experts recommend seeking assistance from cybersecurity professionals or specialized malware removal services when dealing with Trojan infections.

In summary, Trojans are a pervasive and deceptive category of malware that relies on social engineering and user interaction to infiltrate and compromise systems.

Their versatility and ability to evolve make them a constant threat in the ever-changing cybersecurity landscape.

To protect against Trojans effectively, a layered security approach, user education, and proactive monitoring are essential components of a comprehensive cybersecurity strategy.

Being vigilant and staying informed about the latest Trojan threats and attack techniques is crucial in defending against these insidious cyber threats.

Chapter 3: Anatomy of a Trojan Horse

To understand the inner workings of a Trojan, it's essential to dissect its various components, each playing a distinct role in carrying out malicious activities. Trojans are like digital chameleons, camouflaging themselves as legitimate software while concealing their nefarious objectives.

The first and most crucial component of a Trojan is the "Loader" or "Downloader." This initial piece of code is responsible for the Trojan's deployment and execution on the victim's system. It often arrives via deceptive email attachments, compromised downloads, or infected software.

Once the Loader is executed, it silently deploys the Trojan on the target system. This component ensures that the Trojan remains hidden from the user and any security software in place. It may use various techniques, such as rootkit functionality or process injection, to evade detection.

The "Command and Control (C2) Server" is another integral part of a Trojan. This server serves as the central communication hub, allowing the attacker to control the infected system remotely. The Trojan establishes a covert connection with the C2 server, enabling the attacker to send commands and receive data from the compromised system.

To maintain persistence and ensure that the Trojan survives system reboots, a "Persistence Mechanism" is often employed. This mechanism can take various forms, such as modifying registry entries, creating scheduled tasks, or installing a service, ensuring that the Trojan remains active and hidden.

"Payload Delivery" is a critical component that determines the specific actions the Trojan will perform on the infected system. The payload can vary widely, depending on the attacker's objectives. Some Trojans are designed to steal sensitive data, while others may grant the attacker full control over the compromised system.

To facilitate the theft of sensitive information, Trojans often include a "Keylogger" component. Keyloggers silently record every keystroke made by the user, capturing sensitive data like usernames, passwords, and credit card numbers. This information is then transmitted to the attacker's C2 server for exploitation.

Another common component found in Trojans is the "Screen Capture" module. This component periodically captures screenshots of the victim's desktop, allowing the attacker to visually monitor the user's activities. This can be particularly useful for capturing sensitive information, such as login credentials or personal messages.

Trojans may also include a "Data Exfiltration" module. This component is responsible for collecting and exfiltrating stolen data to the attacker's server. It can include functionalities like compressing data, encrypting it, and obfuscating the exfiltration process to avoid detection.

To evade detection by security software and analysts, Trojans often employ "Anti-Analysis" techniques. These techniques can include code obfuscation, anti-debugging measures, and polymorphic code generation, making it challenging to analyze and reverse engineer the Trojan.

In some cases, Trojans include "Self-Updating" capabilities. This allows the Trojan to download and install updated versions of itself from the attacker's server, ensuring that it remains current and effective in the face of evolving security measures.

To maximize the impact of a Trojan, some variants incorporate "Propagation Mechanisms." These mechanisms enable the Trojan to spread to other systems, either within the same network or across the internet. Common propagation methods include exploiting software vulnerabilities or using social engineering tactics to trick users into executing the Trojan.

In summary, the components of a Trojan work together seamlessly to carry out various malicious activities, from initial deployment and persistence on the victim's system to data theft and remote control by the attacker. These components are carefully designed and orchestrated to remain hidden and evade detection, making Trojans a formidable threat in the world of cybersecurity.

The successful deployment of Trojans relies heavily on effective delivery and execution mechanisms, which determine how the malicious software gains access to a victim's system and becomes operational.

Delivery mechanisms encompass a wide range of tactics and techniques used by cybercriminals to trick users into installing or executing Trojans unknowingly.

One common delivery method is email phishing, where attackers craft convincing emails that appear to come from trusted sources or organizations.

These emails often contain malicious attachments or links that, when opened or clicked, initiate the download and execution of the Trojan.

Attackers can also use social engineering tactics, such as impersonating tech support or government agencies, to manipulate users into downloading and running the Trojan.

Another delivery mechanism involves the exploitation of software vulnerabilities.

Attackers actively search for security flaws in operating systems, applications, or plugins that can serve as entry points for Trojans.

Once a vulnerability is identified, attackers can deploy the Trojan through methods like drive-by downloads, where users are infected simply by visiting a compromised website.

Social engineering plays a pivotal role in Trojan delivery.

Attackers often create enticing lures, such as fake software updates, free downloads, or enticing offers, to entice users into executing the Trojan.

These deceptive tactics prey on users' curiosity and desire for convenience or gain, increasing the likelihood of successful delivery.

Phishing campaigns, specifically spear-phishing, are highly effective delivery mechanisms for Trojans.

In spear-phishing attacks, attackers target specific individuals or organizations, tailoring their lures to appear personalized and convincing.

This approach often leverages stolen credentials or insider information to gain the victim's trust.

Another method of Trojan delivery involves the use of malicious websites and malicious advertisements, also known as malvertising.

Cybercriminals compromise legitimate websites or ad networks, injecting malicious code that redirects users to sites hosting Trojans.

These websites may appear benign, further deceiving users into executing the Trojan.

For attackers seeking to infiltrate corporate networks, Trojan delivery through compromised supply chains is a prevalent tactic.

Attackers infiltrate trusted software vendors or service providers, embedding Trojans within legitimate software updates or packages.

When organizations unknowingly install these tainted updates, the Trojan gains access to their systems.

Once delivered, the execution mechanism comes into play, enabling the Trojan to run on the victim's system.

The Trojan often arrives in the form of a file, such as an executable (.exe) or a script, which is executed by the operating system.

Command-line interfaces (CLIs) can be leveraged to execute Trojans on the victim's system.

For example, an attacker can use Windows Command Prompt to run a malicious script or binary file, initiating the Trojan's execution.

Similarly, on Linux systems, attackers can use the terminal to execute malicious commands or binaries.

Beyond manual execution, Trojans may employ various auto-start mechanisms to ensure their execution every time the system boots.

These mechanisms can include modifying system settings, creating scheduled tasks, or installing services that initiate the Trojan's execution automatically.

To maintain persistence on the infected system, Trojans often integrate with the system's processes and registry.

They may use rootkit techniques to hide their presence and evade detection by security software.

Some Trojans employ privilege escalation techniques to gain higher levels of access on the victim's system.

This allows them to bypass security restrictions and carry out more sophisticated attacks.

Once the Trojan is successfully executed and operational, it establishes a connection with a command-and-control (C2) server controlled by the attacker.

This connection allows the attacker to remotely control the Trojan, send commands, and receive stolen data.

In summary, the delivery and execution mechanisms of Trojans are multifaceted and dynamic, designed to deceive users and infiltrate systems seamlessly.

These mechanisms encompass a wide range of tactics, including phishing, exploitation of vulnerabilities, social engineering, and malicious websites.

Once delivered, Trojans employ various techniques to execute and maintain persistence, ultimately serving the attacker's malicious objectives.

Understanding these mechanisms is crucial for individuals and organizations seeking to defend against Trojan attacks and bolster their cybersecurity defenses.

Chapter 4: Basic Principles of Cyber Defense

The Defense in Depth strategy is a fundamental approach to cybersecurity, aiming to protect computer systems, networks, and data from a wide range of threats.

This strategy recognizes that a single security measure is insufficient to safeguard against today's evolving and sophisticated cyber threats.

Instead, it advocates for a multi-layered, comprehensive approach that places multiple defensive barriers at different levels within an organization's IT infrastructure.

The primary goal of Defense in Depth is to create redundancy and resilience, ensuring that if one layer of defense is breached, others remain intact to mitigate the impact of an attack.

One essential aspect of Defense in Depth is physical security.

This involves securing the physical premises where computer systems and networking equipment are housed, restricting access to authorized personnel only, and implementing measures like surveillance cameras and alarms.

Physical security helps prevent unauthorized individuals from physically tampering with hardware or gaining access to sensitive areas.

At the network level, firewalls play a crucial role in Defense in Depth.

Firewalls are security devices or software that control incoming and outgoing network traffic based on an organization's previously established security policies.

Firewalls can block or allow traffic based on criteria such as source and destination IP addresses, port numbers, and application protocols.

By configuring firewalls properly, organizations can create a strong first line of defense against external threats.

Intrusion Detection Systems (IDS) and Intrusion Prevention Systems (IPS) are additional network-level security measures that complement Defense in Depth.

IDS monitors network traffic for suspicious or anomalous patterns and generates alerts when potential threats are detected.

IPS, on the other hand, can take immediate action to block or prevent identified threats from entering the network.

Together, IDS and IPS help identify and respond to network-based attacks.

Moving further into the network, access control mechanisms are vital components of Defense in Depth.

These mechanisms include authentication and authorization procedures that ensure only authorized users have access to specific resources or data.

Authentication verifies a user's identity, typically through methods like username and password, biometrics, or multi-factor authentication (MFA).

Authorization determines what actions or resources an authenticated user can access or manipulate.

At the application layer, secure coding practices are crucial for defending against software vulnerabilities and attacks.

Developers must follow best practices to write secure code, perform code reviews, and conduct vulnerability assessments.

Vulnerabilities in software applications can be exploited by attackers, potentially leading to data breaches or system compromises.

Security awareness training is an integral part of Defense in Depth, focusing on educating employees about cybersecurity threats and best practices.

Users are often the weakest link in an organization's security, as social engineering attacks like phishing prey on human psychology and gullibility.

Training helps employees recognize and respond to potential threats, reducing the risk of falling victim to attacks.

Data encryption is a critical component of Defense in Depth, especially for protecting sensitive information.

Encryption algorithms scramble data into an unreadable format, which can only be decrypted with the appropriate encryption key.

Encrypting data at rest, in transit, and during storage helps protect it from unauthorized access even if an attacker gains access to the system or intercepts network traffic.

Regularly updating and patching software and systems is essential for maintaining a strong defense against known vulnerabilities.

Attackers often target outdated or unpatched software, taking advantage of security flaws.

Patching promptly ensures that these vulnerabilities are addressed, reducing the attack surface.

Endpoint security solutions, such as antivirus and anti-malware software, are crucial components of Defense in Depth.

These solutions scan and monitor individual devices, such as computers and smartphones, for malicious software or activities.

They can detect and remove malware, preventing it from spreading across the network.

To further protect against insider threats, organizations can implement security information and event management (SIEM) systems.

SIEM solutions collect and analyze logs and security events from various sources, identifying suspicious activities or deviations from normal behavior.

This helps organizations detect and respond to potential insider threats or unauthorized activities.

Security monitoring and incident response capabilities are key aspects of Defense in Depth.

Organizations should continuously monitor their network and systems for signs of suspicious activity, allowing them to respond quickly to security incidents.

Incident response plans outline procedures for handling and mitigating security breaches.

Finally, regular security audits and penetration testing help organizations assess the effectiveness of their Defense in Depth strategy.

These assessments identify weaknesses and vulnerabilities that require remediation, ensuring that the security posture remains robust and adaptable to evolving threats.

In summary, the Defense in Depth strategy is a holistic approach to cybersecurity that acknowledges the complexity of modern threats.

By implementing multiple layers of defense at various levels within an organization's infrastructure, organizations can create a resilient and comprehensive security posture.

Each layer adds redundancy and protection, reducing the likelihood of successful cyberattacks and minimizing the potential impact of breaches.

While no defense strategy can guarantee absolute security, Defense in Depth provides a strong foundation for safeguarding digital assets and data.

Access control and authentication are integral components of modern cybersecurity, playing a vital role in safeguarding digital resources, sensitive data, and critical systems.

Access control refers to the processes and mechanisms that determine who or what is allowed to access specific resources or perform certain actions within an information system.

It is the first line of defense in preventing unauthorized users or entities from gaining access to sensitive information or compromising the integrity of an organization's digital assets.

Authentication, on the other hand, is the process of verifying the identity of users, devices, or entities attempting to access a system or resource.

Authentication mechanisms ensure that individuals or entities are who they claim to be before granting them access to protected resources.

Access control is achieved through the implementation of access control policies, which define the rules and permissions that govern access to resources.

These policies can specify which users or groups of users have permission to read, write, or execute files, access specific network services, or perform administrative tasks.

In many organizations, access control is typically enforced through user accounts, permissions, and roles.

User accounts are unique identifiers assigned to individuals or entities within a system, enabling them to log in and access resources.

Each user account is associated with specific permissions and privileges, which dictate what actions or resources the user can access.

Permissions are the fine-grained rules that specify the actions or operations a user is allowed to perform on a resource, such as reading, writing, or executing a file.

Roles are predefined sets of permissions that can be assigned to users or groups, simplifying the management of access control policies.

Access control lists (ACLs) are commonly used to define and manage permissions on files, directories, or network resources.

An ACL specifies which users or groups have permission to access or modify a resource and the type of access they are allowed.

For example, a file's ACL may grant read access to a specific user and write access to a group.

In addition to ACLs, discretionary access control (DAC) and mandatory access control (MAC) are two fundamental access control models.

DAC allows resource owners to control access to their resources, granting or revoking permissions at their discretion.

MAC, on the other hand, enforces access control based on security labels or classifications, often used in military or government environments to protect classified information.

Access control can be implemented using various methods and technologies, including role-based access control (RBAC), attribute-based access control (ABAC), and rule-based access control (RuBAC).

RBAC assigns permissions based on a user's role within an organization, simplifying access management.

ABAC considers various attributes, such as user attributes, resource attributes, and environmental attributes, when making access decisions.

RuBAC employs predefined rules to determine access, evaluating conditions and criteria before granting or denying permissions.

Authentication mechanisms are designed to confirm the identity of users or entities before allowing them to access a system or resource.

One of the most common authentication methods is username and password authentication, where users provide a unique username and a secret password.

To access a system or resource, users must correctly enter their credentials during the authentication process.

Multi-factor authentication (MFA) enhances security by requiring users to provide multiple forms of verification.

This can include something they know (a password), something they have (a token or smart card), or something they are (biometric data like fingerprints or facial recognition).

Public key infrastructure (PKI) is another robust authentication method that uses asymmetric cryptography.

Users have a pair of cryptographic keys: a private key kept secret and a public key shared with others.

During authentication, the user presents their public key, and the system verifies it using a corresponding certificate issued by a trusted certificate authority.

Single sign-on (SSO) is an authentication approach that allows users to access multiple systems or applications with a single set of credentials.

SSO enhances user convenience while maintaining security through centralized authentication.

Federated authentication enables users to access resources across multiple domains or organizations using their existing credentials.

This method simplifies access for users and streamlines authentication processes between trusted entities.

Access control and authentication are not only critical for protecting digital resources but also for ensuring compliance with regulatory requirements, safeguarding sensitive data, and mitigating security risks.

Implementing robust access control policies and authentication mechanisms is an ongoing process that requires regular monitoring and updates to adapt to evolving threats and technologies.

To manage access control and authentication effectively, organizations should conduct regular security audits, monitor access logs, and implement intrusion detection systems to identify suspicious activities or unauthorized access attempts.

Additionally, organizations should educate employees about best practices for creating and maintaining strong passwords, recognizing phishing attempts, and safeguarding their authentication credentials.

In summary, access control and authentication are foundational elements of cybersecurity, forming the basis for protecting digital assets and ensuring only authorized users can access sensitive resources.

By implementing robust access control policies and authentication mechanisms, organizations can enhance their security posture, reduce the risk of data breaches, and safeguard critical systems and data.

Chapter 5: Essential Security Tools for Beginners

Antivirus software and endpoint protection are essential components of cybersecurity, serving as a critical defense against a wide range of malicious threats that target individual devices, such as computers and smartphones.

These security tools are designed to detect, prevent, and remove malware, including viruses, Trojans, worms, spyware, and ransomware, that can compromise the security and functionality of endpoints.

The term "endpoint" refers to any device that connects to a network, making it a potential entry point for cyberattacks.

Antivirus software and endpoint protection solutions are particularly vital in today's interconnected world, where digital threats continue to evolve in sophistication and scope.

The core function of antivirus software is to scan files and processes on an endpoint device for signs of malicious code or behavior.

It does this by comparing the data it scans with a database of known malware signatures or patterns.

When a match is found, the antivirus software takes action to quarantine, remove, or neutralize the threat, protecting the device and the data it contains.

In addition to signature-based detection, modern antivirus solutions incorporate heuristic analysis and behavior-based detection techniques.

Heuristic analysis identifies potential threats based on characteristics and behaviors that may indicate malicious intent, even if there is no exact signature match in the database.

Behavior-based detection monitors the activity of files and processes in real-time, looking for suspicious actions or deviations from normal behavior.

Antivirus software also includes features like real-time scanning, which continuously monitors the device for potential threats as files are accessed or executed.

This proactive approach helps detect and prevent malware from compromising the system.

Endpoint protection solutions often include more comprehensive security features beyond traditional antivirus functionality.

These features may encompass firewall protection, intrusion detection and prevention, data loss prevention, and device control.

Firewall protection adds an additional layer of security by monitoring network traffic and blocking or allowing connections based on predefined rules.

Intrusion detection and prevention systems (IDS/IPS) can identify and respond to network-based threats and attacks, helping to safeguard both the device and the network it is connected to.

Data loss prevention (DLP) features help prevent the unauthorized sharing or leakage of sensitive data from the endpoint.

This is particularly important for organizations that need to protect confidential information, such as customer data or intellectual property.

Device control features allow administrators to manage and restrict the use of external devices, such as USB drives and external hard disks, to prevent data breaches or the introduction of malware.

Endpoint protection solutions are often managed through centralized consoles that provide administrators with visibility into the security status of all endpoint devices in the organization.

This centralized management enables administrators to deploy updates, configure security policies, and respond to security incidents efficiently.

To deploy antivirus software and endpoint protection effectively, organizations should follow best practices for implementation.

This includes regularly updating the software to ensure it has the latest malware signatures and security patches.

Endpoint devices should also be kept up-to-date with operating system and software updates to minimize vulnerabilities.

Regular scans and monitoring of endpoint devices are essential to detect and respond to threats promptly.

Users should be educated about the importance of not disabling or circumventing antivirus software, as doing so can leave the device vulnerable to attacks.

When it comes to configuring firewall rules and intrusion detection and prevention settings, organizations should strike a balance between security and usability.

Overly restrictive settings can hinder legitimate network traffic and user activities.

Endpoint protection is not limited to traditional desktop or laptop computers.

With the proliferation of mobile devices, smartphones, and tablets, it has become crucial to extend security measures to all endpoints, regardless of the platform or form factor.

Endpoint protection can be deployed on mobile devices to safeguard against mobile-specific threats, such as mobile malware and phishing attacks targeting mobile users.

In summary, antivirus software and endpoint protection are fundamental tools in the fight against cyber threats that target individual devices.

Their role in detecting and preventing malware, as well as their additional security features, make them vital components of a robust cybersecurity strategy.

As digital threats continue to evolve, organizations must stay vigilant in implementing and maintaining effective antivirus and endpoint protection solutions to protect their endpoints and the data they contain.

Firewalls and Intrusion Detection Systems (IDS) are critical components of network security, serving as the first line of defense against cyber threats and malicious activities.

Firewalls act as a barrier between a trusted internal network and untrusted external networks, such as the internet, by inspecting and controlling incoming and outgoing network traffic.

They operate based on predefined rules and policies, making decisions about whether to allow or block specific network connections or packets based on criteria like source IP address, destination IP address, port numbers, and application protocols.

Firewalls can be deployed at various points within a network architecture, including network perimeter firewalls, which protect the entire network from external threats, and host-based firewalls, which are installed on individual devices to control their network traffic.

Network perimeter firewalls are often the first line of defense, filtering traffic before it reaches the internal network.

Intrusion Detection Systems, on the other hand, are security mechanisms designed to monitor network or system activities for signs of suspicious or potentially malicious behavior.

Unlike firewalls, IDS focus on detecting anomalies and known attack patterns within network traffic or system logs rather than actively blocking or allowing traffic.

There are two main types of IDS: network-based intrusion detection systems (NIDS) and host-based intrusion detection systems (HIDS).

NIDS analyze network traffic in real-time, looking for patterns or behaviors that match known attack signatures or indicators of compromise.

They can be strategically placed at key points within the network to monitor traffic flowing between segments.

HIDS, on the other hand, are deployed on individual hosts or endpoints, where they monitor system logs and activities specific to that device.

HIDS are effective at detecting suspicious activities that may not be apparent at the network level, such as local privilege escalations or unauthorized file modifications.

Firewalls and IDS often work in tandem to provide comprehensive network security.

Firewalls filter incoming and outgoing traffic, blocking known threats and enforcing network policies, while IDS analyze traffic and system activities to identify potential threats or security breaches.

To configure a firewall, administrators typically define a set of rules and policies that specify which traffic is allowed or blocked.

For example, a firewall rule may allow incoming web traffic (HTTP) on port 80 but block incoming remote desktop (RDP) traffic on port 3389.

Firewall rules can be configured using command-line interface (CLI) commands or through graphical user interfaces (GUIs) provided by firewall management software.

For instance, in a Cisco ASA firewall, administrators can use the CLI to create an access control list (ACL) rule like this:

```
arduinoCopy code
access-list outside_access_in extended permit tcp any host 192.168.1.10 eq 80
```

This rule allows incoming TCP traffic on port 80 (HTTP) from any source IP address to the internal host with IP address 192.168.1.10.

Intrusion Detection Systems, whether network-based or host-based, rely on a combination of signature-based detection and anomaly-based detection.

Signature-based detection involves comparing network traffic or system events against a database of known attack patterns or signatures.

If a match is found, the IDS generates an alert.

Anomaly-based detection, on the other hand, establishes a baseline of normal network or system behavior and triggers alerts when deviations from this baseline are detected.

For example, an IDS may generate an alert if an excessive number of failed login attempts occur within a short time frame.

IDS alerts are typically logged and can be configured to trigger notifications to security administrators or analysts.

These alerts provide valuable information about potential security incidents, allowing organizations to respond promptly to threats.

Firewalls and IDS are essential components of a layered security approach known as Defense in Depth.

By combining these technologies with other security measures such as antivirus software, access control, and regular security audits, organizations can create a robust and adaptive security posture to defend against a wide range of cyber threats.

In summary, firewalls and Intrusion Detection Systems are foundational elements of network security, working together to protect against unauthorized access, data breaches, and malicious activities.

Their roles in filtering and monitoring network traffic, as well as identifying suspicious behavior, make them indispensable tools in the ongoing battle against cyber threats.

To deploy and configure these security mechanisms effectively, organizations must develop clear policies and procedures, stay informed about emerging threats, and regularly update and test their security infrastructure.

Chapter 6: Internet Safety and Best Practices

Safe browsing habits are essential for maintaining a secure and enjoyable online experience, as the internet is a vast and dynamic environment that presents various risks and threats.

By adopting responsible and proactive browsing practices, individuals can protect themselves and their digital assets from cyberattacks, scams, and privacy breaches.

One fundamental aspect of safe browsing is keeping software and operating systems up to date, as software updates often include security patches that address known vulnerabilities.

For example, in a Windows environment, individuals can use the Windows Update feature to ensure their system is receiving the latest security updates:

mathematicaCopy code

Windows Update

Similarly, on macOS, the Software Update feature serves the same purpose:

sqlCopy code

Apple menu > System Preferences > Software Update

Regularly updating web browsers, browser extensions, and plugins is also crucial.

Browsers like Google Chrome and Mozilla Firefox frequently release updates that improve security and stability.

Users can check for updates in their browsers' settings or by typing "chrome://settings/help" in the address bar for Chrome or "about:preferences#general" for Firefox.

To enhance security while browsing, it's advisable to use strong and unique passwords for online accounts.

Password management tools like LastPass or 1Password can help individuals generate and securely store complex passwords:

arduinoCopy code

Install LastPass: https://www.lastpass.com/

Moreover, enabling two-factor authentication (2FA) whenever possible adds an extra layer of security to online accounts.

Two-factor authentication requires users to provide a second form of verification, such as a temporary code sent to their mobile device, in addition to their password.

While browsing the web, it's essential to exercise caution when clicking on links or downloading files.

Users should verify the legitimacy of websites and ensure they are using secure connections by looking for the padlock icon in the browser's address bar, indicating an SSL/TLS-encrypted connection.

Avoiding suspicious websites and refraining from clicking on unsolicited email attachments or links in emails from unknown senders can prevent malware infections and phishing attempts.

Phishing is a deceptive technique used by cybercriminals to trick users into revealing sensitive information or installing malicious software.

When downloading files or software from the internet, users should rely on trusted sources and verify the authenticity of the download.

For example, downloading software from the official website or an authorized distributor is generally safer than downloading from third-party sources.

Additionally, users can verify file integrity by comparing the provided checksum with the calculated checksum of the downloaded file.

To perform a checksum verification on a downloaded file in a Linux terminal, users can use the following command, replacing "file.tar.gz" with the actual file name and checksum:

bashCopy code

```
sha256sum file.tar.gz
```

For added privacy and security while browsing, consider using a virtual private network (VPN).

A VPN encrypts internet traffic, making it more challenging for third parties to monitor online activities or track users' locations.

Popular VPN services like NordVPN or ExpressVPN offer both free and paid options.

Protecting personal information and privacy online is paramount.

Users should be cautious about sharing sensitive data, such as Social Security numbers, credit card information, and home addresses, on websites or with unknown individuals or organizations.

Regularly reviewing privacy settings on social media platforms and other online accounts is also advisable.

Many websites offer granular control over what information is shared with others and how personal data is used.

Online shopping and financial transactions require extra vigilance.

Before making a purchase on an e-commerce website, users should ensure that the website is secure by checking for the padlock symbol and verifying the legitimacy of the website's SSL/TLS certificate.

Furthermore, users should refrain from entering sensitive information on public or unsecured Wi-Fi networks, as these networks may not encrypt data, making it vulnerable to interception.

To bolster online security, consider using browser extensions or add-ons that provide additional protection against malicious websites and online threats.

For instance, browser extensions like "uBlock Origin" can block unwanted ads and malicious scripts:

rubyCopy code

Install uBlock Origin for Chrome:
https://chrome.google.com/webstore/detail/ublock-origin/cjpalhdlnbpafiamejdnhcphjbkeiagm

Regularly clearing browser cookies and cache can help protect privacy and reduce the risk of tracking by advertisers and third-party entities.

Browser settings usually provide options for managing cookies and cached data.

Safe browsing habits extend to email practices as well.

Be cautious when opening email attachments or clicking on links in emails, even if they appear to be from a known sender.

Cybercriminals often use email as a vector for malware distribution or phishing attacks.

To enhance email security, consider using email encryption tools or secure email services.

Tools like PGP (Pretty Good Privacy) can encrypt email content and attachments to prevent unauthorized access:

javaCopy code

Install Gpg4win (PGP encryption software for Windows): https://gpg4win.org/

In summary, safe browsing habits are essential for protecting oneself and one's digital presence in an increasingly interconnected world.

By staying informed about online threats, regularly updating software, using strong passwords and two-factor authentication, and exercising caution when interacting with websites and emails, individuals can significantly reduce their exposure to cyber risks.

Cultivating these habits can lead to a more secure and enjoyable online experience while safeguarding personal information and digital assets.

Email security is a paramount concern in the digital age, as email remains a primary communication tool for individuals and organizations, but it also represents a significant vector for cyberattacks and phishing attempts.

Phishing is a malicious technique used by cybercriminals to trick recipients into divulging sensitive information, clicking on malicious links, or downloading malicious attachments through deceptive emails.

To mitigate email security risks and protect against phishing, it is essential to understand the various aspects of email security and develop a high level of phishing awareness.

One of the fundamental elements of email security is encryption, which ensures that email content remains confidential and is only accessible to intended recipients.

Encryption mechanisms, such as Transport Layer Security (TLS), protect the email communication during transit, preventing eavesdropping by unauthorized parties.

Users can enhance email encryption by using end-to-end encryption tools, such as Pretty Good Privacy (PGP), to encrypt the content of their emails.

PGP requires the use of public and private keys, which users generate and manage.

To send an encrypted email using PGP, one can use the following CLI command:

cssCopy code

```
gpg --encrypt --recipient recipient@example.com my_message.txt
```

This command encrypts the content of "my_message.txt" using the recipient's public key and generates an encrypted email that only the recipient can decrypt with their private key.

Additionally, organizations can implement email filtering and spam detection solutions to automatically identify and quarantine malicious or suspicious emails.

These solutions analyze email content, attachments, sender reputation, and other factors to classify emails as spam or potential threats.

Users should be cautious about downloading email attachments or clicking on links within emails, especially if the email originates from an unknown or untrusted source.

Before taking any action, it is advisable to verify the authenticity of the sender and the legitimacy of the email.

Phishing awareness is crucial in recognizing and thwarting phishing attempts.

Users should be cautious about emails that request sensitive information, such as passwords, Social Security numbers, or credit card details, as legitimate organizations typically do not solicit such information via email.

Furthermore, phishing emails often contain urgency or pressure tactics, such as threatening account suspension or promising unexpected rewards, to manipulate recipients into taking quick actions.

To illustrate a common phishing scenario, consider an email that appears to be from a reputable bank, claiming that the recipient's account has been compromised and requesting immediate login credentials.

In this situation, users should not click on any links or download attachments from the email.

Instead, they should independently verify the authenticity of the email by contacting the bank through official channels, such as a phone number from the bank's official website or a physical branch.

Another form of phishing is spear phishing, which targets specific individuals or organizations with highly personalized and convincing messages.

Spear phishing emails may appear to come from colleagues, superiors, or trusted partners and often contain details specific to the recipient's role or relationships.

Phishing awareness training can help individuals recognize common phishing tactics and learn how to respond effectively.

Training programs provide guidance on identifying suspicious emails, avoiding interaction with phishing attempts, and reporting incidents to IT or security teams.

In organizations, it is essential to establish clear email security policies and procedures to govern email usage and protect sensitive data.

These policies can specify guidelines for handling sensitive information, reporting suspicious emails, and ensuring that email communications adhere to security best practices.

Additionally, implementing email authentication mechanisms, such as Domain-based Message Authentication, Reporting, and Conformance (DMARC) and Sender Policy Framework (SPF), can help prevent email spoofing and domain impersonation.

DMARC and SPF records are added to the DNS configuration of an email domain and specify which servers are authorized to send email on behalf of the domain.

To check for the presence of SPF records, users can use the "nslookup" command in a CLI:

bashCopy code

```
nslookup -type=txt example.com
```

This command queries the DNS records of "example.com" to retrieve SPF records, which indicate which servers are authorized to send email on behalf of the domain.

Moreover, implementing strong email authentication and access controls, such as multi-factor authentication (MFA) and strong password policies, can further enhance email security.

MFA requires users to provide two or more verification factors, such as something they know (password), something they have (smartphone or token), or something they are (biometric data) to access their email accounts.

Phishing awareness extends to mobile devices, where users should exercise the same caution when opening emails and clicking on links.

Mobile email apps often provide security features like email filtering and spam detection, which users should enable for added protection.

Email security is an ongoing effort that requires individuals and organizations to stay vigilant, adapt to evolving threats, and keep email systems and software up to date.

By combining encryption, email filtering, phishing awareness, and authentication mechanisms, users can maintain a high level of email security and reduce the risk of falling victim to phishing attacks.

Education and training are critical components of email security, as they empower individuals to recognize and respond effectively to email threats, ultimately enhancing the overall security posture of individuals and organizations in the digital age.

Chapter 7: Securing Your Devices and Networks

Device hardening techniques are essential practices in cybersecurity aimed at enhancing the security posture of computers, servers, and other devices by reducing vulnerabilities and minimizing attack surfaces.

Hardening devices involves configuring and managing various aspects of the operating system, software, and hardware to mitigate risks and protect against potential threats.

One crucial step in device hardening is applying security updates and patches regularly.

Operating system vendors and software developers release updates to address known vulnerabilities and weaknesses, so it is vital to keep devices up to date with the latest security fixes.

To update a Linux-based system, users can utilize the "apt-get" command for Debian-based distributions or "yum" for Red Hat-based distributions:

sqlCopy code

```
sudo apt-get update sudo apt-get upgrade
```

Similarly, on Windows systems, users can use the "Windows Update" feature to install the latest updates and security patches.

Another device hardening practice is to disable unnecessary services and features that are not required for the device's intended function.

By reducing the attack surface, potential avenues for exploitation are minimized.

On Linux systems, administrators can use the "systemctl" command to disable specific services from starting at boot:

bashCopy code

```
sudo systemctl disable <service-name>
```

In Windows, services can be disabled through the "Services" application in the Control Panel.

Limiting user privileges is a crucial aspect of device hardening. Users should only have the minimum level of access and permissions required to perform their tasks.

This principle, known as the principle of least privilege (PoLP), helps prevent unauthorized access and privilege escalation.

In Linux, administrators can create and manage user accounts with specific privileges using the "useradd" and "usermod" commands:

phpCopy code

```
sudo useradd -m -G <group> <username>
```

In Windows, user privileges can be configured through the "Local Users and Groups" tool in the Computer Management console.

Implementing strong password policies is vital for device hardening.

Passwords should be complex, regularly changed, and not easily guessable.

Multi-factor authentication (MFA) can be employed to add an extra layer of security.

On Linux, administrators can configure password policies using the "passwd" command:

phpCopy code

```
sudo passwd <username>
```

In Windows, password policies are configured through the Group Policy Editor.

Firewalls are crucial for device hardening, as they help control network traffic and protect against unauthorized access.

Firewalls can be implemented at the network level (hardware firewalls) or on the device itself (software firewalls).

To configure a software firewall on a Linux system, administrators can use the "ufw" (Uncomplicated Firewall) tool:

phpCopy code

```
sudo ufw enable sudo ufw allow <port>/<protocol>
```

For Windows, the built-in Windows Firewall can be configured through the Control Panel.

Regularly monitoring and auditing device logs is another device hardening technique.

Logs provide valuable information about system activities, user actions, and potential security incidents.

By analyzing logs, administrators can detect anomalies and respond promptly to security threats.

In Linux, logs are typically stored in the "/var/log" directory and can be viewed using tools like "cat," "tail," or "grep."

bashCopy code

```
cat /var/log/auth.log
```

Windows event logs can be accessed through the Event Viewer application.

Disk encryption is a crucial aspect of device hardening for protecting data at rest.

Full disk encryption (FDE) ensures that if a device is lost or stolen, the data stored on it remains inaccessible without the encryption passphrase or key.

On Linux, administrators can use tools like "LUKS" (Linux Unified Key Setup) for disk encryption during installation or afterward:

bashCopy code

```
sudo cryptsetup luksFormat /dev/sdX sudo cryptsetup open /dev/sdX myencrypteddisk
```

For Windows, BitLocker provides disk encryption capabilities and can be configured through the Control Panel.

Regular backups are an essential device hardening practice to ensure data can be recovered in the event of data loss or ransomware attacks.

Backups should be stored securely and regularly tested for restoration.

To perform a backup on a Linux system, administrators can use tools like "rsync" or dedicated backup solutions:

bashCopy code

```
rsync -av /source-directory /backup-directory
```

In Windows, the built-in Backup and Restore tool can be used for creating backups.

Implementing network segmentation is a device hardening technique that separates a network into smaller, isolated segments.

This helps contain potential breaches and prevents lateral movement by attackers.

On Linux, network segmentation can be achieved using tools like "iptables" to create firewall rules:

phpCopy code

```
sudo iptables -A FORWARD -s <source-ip> -d <destination-ip> -j DROP
```

For Windows, network segmentation can be configured through the Windows Firewall.

Device hardening also involves keeping an inventory of devices, software, and configurations.

This helps ensure that devices are properly maintained, monitored, and updated.

Regular vulnerability assessments and penetration testing can identify weaknesses in device configurations and security measures.

By conducting these assessments, organizations can proactively address vulnerabilities before they are exploited by attackers.

Device hardening is an ongoing process that requires continuous monitoring and adjustment as new threats emerge and technologies evolve.

By implementing these techniques, organizations and individuals can significantly improve their device security, reduce the risk of data breaches, and protect against a wide range of cyber threats.

It is essential to stay informed about the latest security best practices and maintain a proactive stance towards device security in today's ever-evolving digital landscape.

Network security measures are critical components of a

comprehensive cybersecurity strategy, aimed at safeguarding an organization's data, systems, and communication channels from various threats and vulnerabilities.

In today's interconnected world, where businesses and individuals rely heavily on networks and the internet for communication and data sharing, the importance of robust network security cannot be overstated.

One fundamental aspect of network security is access control, which involves defining and enforcing rules and policies to determine who can access network resources and what level of access they are granted.

Access control can be managed through user authentication, authorization, and accounting mechanisms.

To configure user access control on a Linux-based network, administrators can use the "sudo" command to grant specific users or groups elevated privileges for performing tasks or accessing resources:

Copy code

```
sudo visudo
```

This command opens the sudoers file, where administrators can define access control rules.

Firewalls play a pivotal role in network security by controlling incoming and outgoing network traffic based on predefined rules and policies.

Firewalls can be deployed at various network levels, such as network perimeter firewalls, host-based firewalls, and application-layer firewalls.

To configure a network perimeter firewall, organizations often use dedicated firewall appliances or software solutions.

For instance, on a Cisco ASA firewall, administrators can use the "access-list" command to define access control rules:

arduinoCopy code

```
access-list outside_access_in extended permit tcp any host 192.168.1.10 eq 80
```

This command allows incoming TCP traffic on port 80 (HTTP) to reach the internal host with IP address 192.168.1.10.

Intrusion Detection Systems (IDS) and Intrusion Prevention Systems (IPS) are crucial network security measures designed to monitor network traffic for signs of suspicious or malicious activity.

IDS passively analyze network traffic and generate alerts when they detect potential threats, while IPS can take active measures to block or prevent these threats.

To configure IDS/IPS rules, organizations typically use specialized security appliances or software solutions that provide a range of predefined rules and the ability to create custom rules based on specific network requirements.

Secure Socket Layer (SSL) and Transport Layer Security (TLS) are cryptographic protocols that ensure the security and privacy of data exchanged between clients and servers over the internet.

SSL and TLS are essential for encrypting data in transit, protecting it from eavesdropping and interception.

To enable SSL/TLS encryption on a web server, administrators can generate a certificate signing request (CSR) and obtain a digital certificate from a trusted certificate authority (CA).

The "openssl" command can be used to generate a CSR:

```
csharpCopy code
openssl req -new -newkey rsa:2048 -nodes -keyout example.com.key -out example.com.csr
```

This command generates a private key and a CSR for the domain "example.com."

Effective network security measures also include continuous monitoring and logging of network activities.

Network administrators should regularly review logs to detect anomalies, track user activities, and identify potential security incidents.

Log management and analysis tools help organizations centralize and analyze log data from various network devices and systems, allowing for rapid incident detection and response.

Additionally, network segmentation is a network security practice that involves dividing a network into smaller, isolated segments to limit the impact of security breaches and unauthorized access.

This technique helps prevent lateral movement by attackers and contains potential breaches to specific network segments.

To segment a network, administrators can use virtual LANs (VLANs) or physical network segmentation, ensuring that different segments have restricted access to one another.

Another essential network security measure is the implementation of security policies and procedures.

These policies provide guidelines and best practices for network configuration, user behavior, data handling, incident response, and more.

Security policies should be documented, regularly reviewed, and enforced across the organization to maintain a consistent security posture.

Network security assessments, including vulnerability scanning and penetration testing, are critical for identifying and addressing weaknesses in network infrastructure and configurations.

These assessments help organizations proactively mitigate vulnerabilities before they can be exploited by attackers.

Vulnerability scanning tools, such as Nessus or OpenVAS, can automatically scan a network for known vulnerabilities:

arduinoCopy code

```
sudo apt-get install openvas
```

This command installs OpenVAS on a Linux system for conducting vulnerability scans.

Penetration testing, on the other hand, involves ethical hackers attempting to exploit vulnerabilities in a controlled environment to assess security weaknesses.

Network security measures also encompass the deployment of intrusion prevention systems (IPS) to actively monitor and block malicious network traffic.

IPS systems can identify and respond to threats by blocking traffic from known malicious IP addresses or patterns of suspicious behavior.

To configure an IPS, organizations can use dedicated appliances or software solutions that provide real-time threat detection and response capabilities.

Network security also extends to wireless networks, where additional measures are needed to protect against unauthorized access and attacks.

Securing wireless networks involves configuring strong authentication protocols, such as WPA3, using strong encryption, and regularly changing default passwords on wireless access points. Network segmentation is essential in wireless environments as well, as it helps isolate guest networks from internal networks, limiting potential threats.

In summary, network security measures are vital for safeguarding networks and the data they transmit from a wide range of threats and vulnerabilities.

These measures encompass access control, firewalls, intrusion detection and prevention systems, encryption, network segmentation, log monitoring, security policies, security assessments, intrusion prevention systems, and wireless network security practices.

By implementing a combination of these measures and staying informed about emerging threats and best practices, organizations can maintain a robust network security posture and reduce the risk of security breaches and data loss.

In today's digital landscape, where cyber threats are continually evolving, network security remains an ongoing and critical endeavor that requires vigilance and proactive measures to protect valuable assets and maintain business continuity.

Chapter 8: Identifying and Responding to Trojan Attacks

Detecting Trojan activity is a critical aspect of cybersecurity, as Trojans are malicious software programs that often go undetected while infiltrating systems and compromising data.

Trojans are notorious for their ability to disguise themselves as legitimate files or software, making their detection challenging.

One of the primary methods for detecting Trojan activity is to deploy antivirus and anti-malware software on all systems within an organization.

These security tools regularly scan files and system memory for known Trojan signatures and behaviors.

To install antivirus software on a Windows computer, users can follow these steps:

Download the antivirus software installer from the official website.

Run the installer and follow the on-screen instructions.

Once installed, perform a full system scan to detect and remove any Trojans or malware.

On Linux-based systems, ClamAV is a popular open-source antivirus solution that can be installed using package managers:
arduinoCopy code

```
sudo apt-get install clamav
```

After installation, users can update the antivirus database and perform scans:
Copy code

```
sudo freshclam clamscan -r /
```

These commands update the virus database and scan the entire file system for malware.

In addition to antivirus software, organizations should employ intrusion detection systems (IDS) and intrusion prevention systems (IPS) to detect and respond to suspicious network and system activity.

IDS and IPS analyze network traffic and system logs to identify patterns and behaviors indicative of Trojan activity.

To deploy an IDS/IPS solution, organizations can choose from a variety of commercial and open-source options, such as Snort or Suricata.

These tools require configuration to define rules and policies for detecting and responding to suspicious network activity.

Regularly monitoring network traffic using network analysis tools is another technique for detecting Trojan activity.

Wireshark is a widely used open-source network protocol analyzer that allows users to capture and analyze network packets in real-time.

To use Wireshark, individuals can download and install it from the official website, then capture network traffic on the desired network interface.

Wireshark provides features for filtering and analyzing traffic, helping users identify suspicious or anomalous behavior.

Behavioral analysis is a powerful method for detecting Trojans that may evade signature-based detection.

This technique involves monitoring the behavior of running processes and system activities to identify deviations from normal operations.

Tools like Sysinternals Process Explorer on Windows or "pstree" on Linux can assist in monitoring processes and their behavior.

For example, on Linux, users can run the following command to view the process tree:

Copy code

```
pstree
```

Processes with unusual names or behavior may warrant further investigation.

File integrity monitoring (FIM) is another technique for detecting Trojan activity.

FIM tools continuously monitor and compare file attributes, such as checksums or timestamps, to detect unauthorized changes.

On Linux systems, the "tripwire" utility is an example of a FIM tool:

arduinoCopy code

```
sudo apt-get install tripwire
```

After installation, users must initialize the database and create a policy file:

cssCopy code

```
sudo tripwire --init sudo tripwire --update-policy
```

Regularly updating the FIM database and checking for policy violations helps detect file-level changes indicative of Trojan activity.

Network traffic analysis using intrusion detection and prevention systems (IDS/IPS) is an effective method for identifying Trojans that communicate with command and control servers or exfiltrate data.

IDS/IPS solutions, such as Snort or Suricata, can be configured to monitor network traffic for suspicious patterns and known malicious IP addresses.

For example, in Snort, administrators can create custom rules to detect specific Trojan behaviors:

cssCopy code

```
alert tcp any any -> $HOME_NET any (msg:"Possible Trojan
Activity";      flow:to_server,established;      content:"GET
/evil.php"; sid:1000001;)
```

This rule triggers an alert when it detects HTTP traffic to a suspicious URL.

User and entity behavior analytics (UEBA) is an advanced method for detecting Trojan activity that relies on machine learning and artificial intelligence algorithms.

UEBA solutions analyze user and entity behavior to identify deviations from normal patterns, flagging potentially malicious activity.

These solutions can detect insider threats and advanced persistent threats that may involve Trojan infections.

Security information and event management (SIEM) systems are powerful tools for detecting Trojan activity by aggregating and correlating data from various sources, such as logs, network traffic, and system activity.

SIEM solutions, like Splunk or ELK Stack, can centralize and analyze vast amounts of data to detect anomalies and generate alerts.

SIEM configuration involves defining correlation rules and log sources to enhance detection capabilities.

Implementing email security solutions can help detect Trojan activity delivered through email attachments or links.

Email security gateways and spam filters can scan incoming emails for malicious attachments, known Trojan signatures, and suspicious URLs.

Advanced email security solutions can also perform sandboxing to analyze and detonate suspicious attachments in a controlled environment.

To illustrate, organizations can deploy email security appliances or cloud-based email security services that offer real-time scanning and protection against email-based threats.

Anomalous network behavior detection is another advanced technique for detecting Trojan activity.

By establishing a baseline of normal network behavior, organizations can identify deviations that may indicate a Trojan infection or network intrusion.

Security teams can use machine learning algorithms and network behavior analysis tools to continuously monitor and detect anomalies.

Implementing a robust incident response plan is crucial for detecting Trojan activity and responding effectively to security incidents.

The incident response plan should outline procedures for identifying, isolating, and mitigating Trojan infections.

Additionally, organizations should conduct regular tabletop exercises and simulations to test the effectiveness of their incident response procedures.

Endpoint detection and response (EDR) solutions are specialized security tools designed for detecting and responding to advanced threats, including Trojans, at the endpoint level.

EDR solutions provide real-time visibility into endpoint activities and behaviors, allowing security teams to detect and respond to suspicious activity promptly.

Organizations can deploy EDR agents on endpoints to monitor and collect data on system activities and network communications.

In summary, detecting Trojan activity requires a multifaceted approach that combines signature-based detection, behavioral analysis, network traffic analysis, file integrity monitoring, and advanced security solutions.

By implementing a combination of these techniques and tools, organizations can significantly improve their ability to detect Trojans and other malicious activities.

It is essential to continuously update and adapt detection methods to keep up with evolving Trojan threats, making detection a critical component of a proactive cybersecurity strategy.

Incident response and mitigation are critical components of a robust cybersecurity strategy, essential for minimizing the impact of security incidents and swiftly restoring normal operations.

Incident response is the systematic process of identifying, managing, and resolving security incidents, which can range from data breaches and malware infections to unauthorized access and insider threats.

When a security incident occurs, organizations must have a well-defined incident response plan in place to ensure a coordinated and effective response.

The incident response plan outlines roles, responsibilities, procedures, and communication protocols for addressing security incidents.

To develop an incident response plan, organizations can use templates and guidelines provided by cybersecurity frameworks like NIST or ISO/IEC 27001.

Incident response plans should include clear incident classification criteria to assess the severity and impact of security incidents.

Incident classification helps prioritize incident response efforts and allocate resources appropriately.

Common incident classification levels include low, medium, high, and critical, each with predefined response procedures and escalation paths.

Once an incident is detected and classified, the incident response team should initiate the response process promptly.

The first step is containment, which involves isolating the affected systems or networks to prevent further damage or data loss.

Containment measures may include disconnecting compromised systems from the network, blocking malicious IP addresses, or quarantining affected users.

On Windows systems, administrators can disable network adapters using the "netsh" command:

vbnetCopy code

```
netsh interface set interface "Local Area Connection" admin=disable
```

This command disables the network adapter named "Local Area Connection."

After containment, organizations should focus on eradication, which involves identifying and eliminating the root cause of the incident.

This step often requires thorough malware analysis, vulnerability assessment, and system forensics to ensure that all malicious components are removed from the affected systems.

To eradicate malware on a Windows system, administrators can use antivirus software or specialized malware removal tools.

The next phase in incident response is recovery, where organizations work to restore affected systems and services to normal operation.

Recovery may involve reinstalling operating systems, restoring data from backups, and applying security patches to prevent future incidents.

Organizations should maintain comprehensive backups of critical data and systems to facilitate the recovery process.

Regularly testing backups is crucial to ensure their reliability in case of an incident.

To back up data on a Linux system, administrators can use the "rsync" command to copy files and directories to a backup location:

bashCopy code

```
rsync -av /source-directory /backup-directory
```

This command creates a backup of the source directory in the specified backup location.

The final phase of incident response is lessons learned and documentation, where organizations conduct a post-incident analysis to identify areas for improvement and document the incident response process.

This phase helps organizations refine their incident response plan and enhance their overall cybersecurity posture.

Incident documentation should include a detailed timeline of events, actions taken, and outcomes.

Additionally, organizations should communicate the incident's impact and resolution to relevant stakeholders, including customers, employees, and regulatory authorities, as required by data breach notification laws.

While the incident response process is crucial, organizations should also prioritize incident mitigation strategies to reduce the likelihood and severity of future incidents.

One of the fundamental mitigation techniques is vulnerability management, which involves identifying, assessing, and remediating security vulnerabilities in systems and software.

Vulnerability scanning tools, such as Nessus or OpenVAS, can automatically scan systems for known vulnerabilities:

arduinoCopy code

```
sudo apt-get install openvas
```

This command installs OpenVAS on a Linux system for conducting vulnerability scans.

Organizations should establish a regular patch management process to apply security updates and patches promptly.

Patch management ensures that systems are protected against known vulnerabilities and reduces the attack surface.

To update a Linux system, administrators can use package managers like "apt" for Debian-based distributions or "yum" for Red Hat-based distributions:

sqlCopy code

```
sudo apt-get update sudo apt-get upgrade
```

For Windows systems, administrators can use the "Windows Update" feature to install security updates and patches.

Another mitigation technique is the use of security information and event management (SIEM) systems to monitor and analyze network and system logs.

SIEM solutions, such as Splunk or ELK Stack, can correlate and alert on suspicious activities, enabling organizations to respond proactively to potential threats.

Implementing a robust identity and access management (IAM) strategy is critical for mitigating unauthorized access and insider threats.

IAM solutions help organizations manage user access, enforce strong authentication, and implement role-based access control (RBAC) to limit privileges.

Organizations should regularly review user access rights and deactivate or modify accounts for employees who no longer require access.

Strong password policies and multi-factor authentication (MFA) are essential components of IAM.

To configure MFA on a Linux-based system, administrators can use the "google-authenticator" tool:

arduinoCopy code

```
sudo apt-get install libpam-google-authenticator
```

This command installs the Google Authenticator module for PAM (Pluggable Authentication Module).

Implementing network segmentation is another effective mitigation technique that limits the lateral movement of attackers within a network.

Network segmentation isolates critical systems and data from less secure areas, making it more challenging for attackers to move laterally and access sensitive resources.

Network segmentation can be achieved using VLANs (Virtual LANs) or dedicated firewalls.

Regular employee training and security awareness programs are crucial for mitigating social engineering attacks and phishing attempts.

Employees should be educated on recognizing phishing emails, suspicious links, and social engineering tactics.

Simulated phishing exercises can help organizations assess employee readiness and improve security awareness.

Additionally, organizations should establish an incident response team with well-defined roles and responsibilities to ensure a coordinated and effective response to incidents.

The incident response team should include representatives from IT, security, legal, and communication departments.

Periodic tabletop exercises and incident response drills can help the team practice and refine their incident response procedures.

In summary, incident response and mitigation are essential components of a comprehensive cybersecurity strategy that organizations must implement to address security incidents effectively and reduce their impact.

Incident response involves detection, containment, eradication, recovery, and lessons learned, with documentation being a crucial part of the process.

Mitigation techniques include vulnerability management, patch management, SIEM implementation, identity and access management, network segmentation, employee training, and incident response preparedness.

By implementing these techniques and fostering a culture of cybersecurity awareness, organizations can proactively manage security incidents and strengthen their overall cybersecurity posture in an ever-evolving threat landscape.

Chapter 9: Building a Foundation for Cyber Hygiene

Password management and authentication practices play a pivotal role in ensuring the security of digital accounts and sensitive information.

Passwords are widely used as a means of verifying user identities and granting access to various systems and services.

However, weak passwords and poor password management are significant contributors to security breaches and unauthorized access incidents.

Therefore, organizations and individuals must adopt effective password management practices to protect their digital assets.

One fundamental password management practice is the creation of strong and complex passwords.

Strong passwords are difficult for attackers to guess or crack through brute-force attacks.

To create strong passwords, consider using a combination of uppercase and lowercase letters, numbers, and special characters.

Avoid using easily guessable information such as birthdays, names, or common words.

An example of a strong password might be "P@$$w0rd#Secure21."

Another essential practice is to avoid password reuse across multiple accounts.

Reusing passwords increases the risk of a security breach because if one account is compromised, all accounts using the same password become vulnerable.

Instead, use unique passwords for each account or service.

To help manage and store complex passwords securely, consider using a password manager application.

Password managers generate and store strong passwords for various accounts, making it easier to maintain strong, unique credentials for each service.

Popular password managers include LastPass, Dashlane, and 1Password.

Password managers typically provide browser extensions and mobile apps for convenient access to stored passwords.

Additionally, many modern operating systems and web browsers offer built-in password management and autofill features.

For instance, Google Chrome's built-in password manager can store and autofill passwords for websites.

To use this feature, simply allow Chrome to save your passwords when prompted and enable autofill in Chrome settings.

However, when using browser-based password managers, be cautious when sharing your computer or device with others, as they may have access to your saved passwords.

Multi-factor authentication (MFA) is a powerful authentication practice that adds an additional layer of security beyond passwords.

MFA requires users to provide two or more authentication factors, typically something they know (password) and something they have (a smartphone or security token).

To enable MFA for an account, navigate to the account's security settings and follow the provided instructions.

Many online services, such as email providers and social media platforms, offer MFA options.

For example, to enable MFA for a Google account, users can visit the Google Account Security page and set up two-factor authentication (2FA) using a mobile app or SMS codes.

Security questions, also known as challenge questions, are commonly used as an additional authentication factor.

However, it's essential to choose challenge questions and answers carefully.

Avoid using easily obtainable information that attackers could find on social media or through research.

Instead, consider using random answers or answers unrelated to the question, as long as you can remember them.

Regularly updating passwords is another crucial practice for maintaining account security.

Even if you have strong passwords and use a password manager, it's essential to change passwords periodically.

To update a password, log in to the respective account or service and navigate to the account settings or security settings.

Follow the instructions to change your password, and ensure the new password is strong and unique.

Many organizations and websites enforce password policies that specify minimum password length, complexity requirements, and expiration intervals.

These policies help ensure that users create and maintain strong passwords.

Password policies often require passwords to be a certain length (e.g., at least eight characters), include a combination of uppercase and lowercase letters, numbers, and special characters, and be changed every 90 days.

Users should adhere to these policies to maintain compliance with organizational or website security requirements.

In addition to maintaining strong and unique passwords, it's vital to be vigilant against phishing attacks.

Phishing is a common technique used by attackers to trick individuals into revealing their login credentials.

Phishing emails often impersonate legitimate organizations and ask users to click on malicious links or provide their username and password.

To protect against phishing attacks, verify the legitimacy of email senders and websites before providing any personal information.

Hover over links in emails to preview the URL before clicking on them.

If you receive an email requesting sensitive information, contact the organization directly through official channels to confirm the request's authenticity.

Many organizations conduct phishing awareness training to educate employees about phishing risks and how to identify phishing attempts.

User education and awareness are essential components of a robust cybersecurity strategy.

Implementing password policies and practices within organizations is equally important.

Organizations should establish and enforce password policies that align with industry best practices.

Password policies should cover password complexity requirements, minimum password lengths, password expiration, and account lockout thresholds.

To enforce password policies, organizations can use group policy settings for Windows domains or utilize third-party identity and access management solutions.

Regularly auditing user accounts for suspicious activity and enforcing account lockout policies help protect against unauthorized access.

When an account breach or compromise is suspected, organizations should promptly investigate the incident, reset passwords, and take corrective actions to prevent future breaches.

In summary, password management and authentication practices are essential for safeguarding digital accounts and sensitive information.

Creating strong and unique passwords, avoiding password reuse, using password managers, and enabling multi-factor authentication are effective ways to enhance account security.

Regularly updating passwords, adhering to password policies, and staying vigilant against phishing attacks are critical for both individuals and organizations.

By adopting these practices, individuals and organizations can significantly reduce the risk of security breaches and protect their valuable digital assets in an increasingly interconnected and digital world.

Software patching and updates are essential elements of cybersecurity and maintaining the integrity and security of computer systems and applications.

Software vendors release patches and updates to address security vulnerabilities, improve functionality, and fix bugs in their products.

These updates play a crucial role in keeping systems protected from emerging threats and ensuring that software operates correctly.

Regularly patching and updating software is a fundamental practice for organizations and individuals alike.

Operating systems, such as Microsoft Windows, macOS, and Linux distributions, require frequent updates to address security vulnerabilities, improve performance, and introduce new features.

To check for and install updates on a Windows system, users can navigate to the "Settings" menu, select "Update & Security," and click on "Check for updates."

Windows will then download and install any available updates.

On macOS, users can access the "Software Update" option in the "System Preferences" menu to check for and install updates.

Linux distributions often use package managers like "apt" (Debian/Ubuntu) or "yum" (Red Hat/CentOS) to manage software updates.

For example, on a Debian-based system, users can run the following commands to update the package list and install available updates:

sqlCopy code

```
sudo apt-get update sudo apt-get upgrade
```

These commands fetch the latest package information and upgrade installed packages to their latest versions.

Web browsers are common targets for cyberattacks, making it crucial to keep them up to date.

Popular browsers like Google Chrome, Mozilla Firefox, and Microsoft Edge release frequent updates to fix security vulnerabilities and improve performance.

To update a web browser, users can visit the browser's settings menu and check for updates or enable automatic updates, which ensures that the browser stays current.

In addition to the operating system and web browser, applications and software packages installed on a system require regular updates.

Application updates often include security patches, bug fixes, and new features.

To manage application updates on Windows, users can use the "Windows Update" feature, which may also include updates for installed Microsoft applications.

On macOS, users can enable automatic updates for Mac App Store applications in the "App Store" settings.

For Linux, application updates are typically managed through the distribution's package manager.

Regularly reviewing and updating installed applications is a proactive measure to maintain system security.

Updating software is not limited to desktop or laptop computers; mobile devices also require regular updates.

Smartphones and tablets use operating systems like Android and iOS, which receive frequent updates to address security issues and provide new features.

To update a mobile device, users can access the device's settings, go to the "Software Update" or "System" section, and check for available updates.

Enabling automatic updates for mobile devices ensures that they receive the latest security patches and feature enhancements.

In addition to keeping software up to date, organizations and individuals should prioritize patching security vulnerabilities as soon as patches become available.

Vulnerability management involves identifying, assessing, and remedying vulnerabilities in software and systems.

Vulnerability scanning tools, such as Nessus or OpenVAS, can automatically scan systems and applications for known vulnerabilities:

arduinoCopy code

```
sudo apt-get install openvas
```

This command installs OpenVAS on a Linux system for conducting vulnerability scans.

Organizations should establish a regular patch management process to apply security updates and patches promptly.

Patch management ensures that systems are protected against known vulnerabilities and reduces the attack surface.

For Linux-based systems, administrators can use package managers like "apt" for Debian-based distributions or "yum" for Red Hat-based distributions to apply security updates.

To update a Debian-based system, administrators can run the following commands:

sqlCopy code

```
sudo apt-get update sudo apt-get upgrade
```

For Windows systems, administrators can use the "Windows Update" feature to install security updates and patches.

Implementing a centralized patch management system can help organizations efficiently deploy updates across their network, ensuring that all systems receive timely patches.

Software patching and updates are essential for addressing known security vulnerabilities.

However, zero-day vulnerabilities are a particular concern because they are exploited by attackers before vendors release patches.

To mitigate the risk of zero-day vulnerabilities, organizations can implement security measures such as intrusion detection systems (IDS) and intrusion prevention systems (IPS) to monitor and block suspicious network traffic.

Additionally, endpoint detection and response (EDR) solutions can provide real-time visibility into endpoint activities, helping organizations detect and respond to advanced threats.

Regularly reviewing and testing backups is essential for disaster recovery and data restoration.

In the event of a security incident or data breach, having up-to-date and secure backups can minimize data loss and downtime.

Backup and recovery solutions should include features like versioning, encryption, and offsite storage to ensure data integrity and availability.

Security information and event management (SIEM) systems play a crucial role in monitoring and alerting organizations about potential security incidents.

SIEM solutions, such as Splunk or ELK Stack, centralize and analyze log data from various sources, including systems, applications, and network devices.

This centralized view helps organizations detect and respond to security events quickly.

When applying software updates and patches, organizations should follow a testing and validation process to ensure that updates do not disrupt critical operations or introduce new vulnerabilities.

Testing patches in a controlled environment before deploying them in production is essential for minimizing the risk of system failures.

In summary, software patching and updates are essential for maintaining the security and functionality of computer systems and applications.

Regularly updating the operating system, web browser, and installed software packages is a fundamental practice for individuals and organizations.

Vulnerability management, patch management, and proactive security measures help mitigate the risk of known and unknown security vulnerabilities.

Implementing security solutions such as IDS, IPS, EDR, and SIEM systems further enhances an organization's ability to detect and respond to security incidents.

By following best practices for software patching and updates, organizations can reduce their exposure to security threats and maintain a strong cybersecurity posture in an ever-evolving threat landscape.

Chapter 10: Cybersecurity Career Pathways for Beginners

Exploring career opportunities in cybersecurity can be an exciting and rewarding journey in today's digital age.

Cybersecurity has become a critical field due to the increasing dependence on technology and the proliferation of cyber threats.

It offers a diverse range of roles and paths for individuals with a passion for protecting information and systems.

One of the most sought-after career paths in cybersecurity is that of a cybersecurity analyst.

Cybersecurity analysts are responsible for monitoring an organization's networks and systems to detect and respond to security incidents.

To pursue a career as a cybersecurity analyst, individuals can start by gaining a strong foundation in networking and security concepts.

They can then pursue relevant certifications such as CompTIA Security+, Certified Information Systems Security Professional (CISSP), or Certified Information Security Manager (CISM).

These certifications validate expertise in cybersecurity and increase employability.

Another promising career option is that of a penetration tester or ethical hacker.

Penetration testers are hired by organizations to simulate cyberattacks on their systems and identify vulnerabilities.

This role requires a deep understanding of computer systems, network protocols, and hacking techniques.

Certifications like Certified Ethical Hacker (CEH) and Offensive Security Certified Professional (OSCP) can provide the necessary skills and knowledge for this career.

For individuals interested in a career focused on protecting sensitive data, a role as a data security analyst might be a good fit.

Data security analysts are responsible for implementing security measures to safeguard data and ensure compliance with data protection regulations.

They work with encryption technologies, access controls, and data loss prevention tools.

To excel in this role, individuals can pursue certifications like Certified Information Systems Security Professional (CISSP) or Certified Information Security Manager (CISM) and gain expertise in data security best practices.

Cybersecurity consultants are professionals who provide expert advice and guidance to organizations on improving their security posture.

They assess vulnerabilities, develop security strategies, and help organizations implement security solutions.

To become a cybersecurity consultant, individuals can acquire a strong background in cybersecurity, gain industry experience, and earn certifications like Certified Information Systems Security Professional (CISSP) or Certified Information Security Manager (CISM).

Another exciting career path in cybersecurity is that of a security architect.

Security architects design and implement security systems and solutions for organizations.

They need a deep understanding of security technologies, risk management, and business processes.

Pursuing certifications like Certified Information Systems Security Professional (CISSP) or Certified Information Security Manager (CISM) can enhance the qualifications for this role.

Incident responders play a critical role in cybersecurity by investigating and mitigating security incidents and breaches.

They must have strong analytical skills and a deep understanding of forensics and incident handling procedures.

Relevant certifications such as Certified Information Systems Security Professional (CISSP) or Certified Incident Handler (GCIH) can be valuable for this career.

In addition to these specific roles, there are also opportunities in cybersecurity management and leadership.

Chief Information Security Officers (CISOs) and security managers are responsible for overseeing an organization's entire cybersecurity program.

They develop security strategies, manage teams, and ensure compliance with regulations.

To reach these leadership positions, individuals can build a solid foundation in cybersecurity, gain experience in progressively responsible roles, and earn relevant certifications.

Cybersecurity offers a wide range of career opportunities not only in traditional corporate settings but also in government agencies, financial institutions, healthcare organizations, and even cybersecurity companies.

Government agencies often hire cybersecurity professionals to protect critical infrastructure and sensitive data.

Financial institutions rely on cybersecurity experts to safeguard customer financial information and prevent fraud.

Healthcare organizations require cybersecurity specialists to protect patient data and ensure compliance with healthcare regulations.

Cybersecurity companies provide specialized security services and solutions to clients, offering diverse roles for professionals in areas like threat intelligence, security software development, and security consulting.

With the increasing demand for cybersecurity professionals, job opportunities continue to grow.

The global shortage of cybersecurity talent has created a job market where skilled individuals are in high demand.

This demand has led to competitive salaries and benefits for cybersecurity professionals, making it an attractive field for those seeking financial stability.

However, a successful career in cybersecurity requires continuous learning and adaptation.

Cyber threats evolve rapidly, and staying current with the latest trends and technologies is essential.

Engaging in professional development through certifications, training, and networking is crucial for career growth.

Networking with other professionals in the field, attending industry conferences, and participating in online forums and communities can provide valuable insights and opportunities.

Additionally, ethical considerations and ethical behavior are paramount in the field of cybersecurity.

Professionals must adhere to ethical guidelines, respect privacy and confidentiality, and prioritize the security and well-being of individuals and organizations.

Cybersecurity professionals also play a crucial role in raising awareness about online safety and educating others about cybersecurity best practices.

Overall, a career in cybersecurity offers not only financial rewards but also the satisfaction of protecting critical information and infrastructure from cyber threats.

It provides an opportunity to make a meaningful impact on the digital landscape and contribute to a safer and more secure online world.

For individuals considering a career in cybersecurity, the path to success involves education, certifications, practical experience, and ongoing learning.

It is a field that welcomes individuals from diverse backgrounds and encourages innovation, problem-solving, and creativity.

With dedication and a commitment to ethical conduct, aspiring cybersecurity professionals can embark on a fulfilling and impactful journey in the world of cybersecurity.

Certifications and education paths are integral components of a successful career in cybersecurity.

They provide the knowledge, skills, and credentials needed to excel in this dynamic and rapidly evolving field.

Cybersecurity certifications are recognized qualifications that validate expertise in various aspects of cybersecurity.

They serve as proof of an individual's proficiency and commitment to the field.

One of the entry-level certifications in cybersecurity is CompTIA Security+.

This certification covers fundamental security concepts, including network security, threats, and risk management.

To earn CompTIA Security+, individuals can prepare for the exam by studying relevant textbooks and taking practice tests.

Additionally, there are many online courses and training programs designed specifically for exam preparation.

For individuals interested in ethical hacking and penetration testing, the Certified Ethical Hacker (CEH) certification is a popular choice.

CEH focuses on offensive security techniques, teaching individuals how to identify vulnerabilities and exploit them responsibly.

To become a Certified Ethical Hacker, candidates must pass the CEH exam, which covers topics like footprinting, scanning, and enumeration.

Preparation for the CEH exam often includes hands-on labs and practical exercises to develop hacking skills.

The Certified Information Systems Security Professional (CISSP) certification is a prestigious credential for experienced security professionals.

CISSP covers a wide range of security domains, including access control, cryptography, and security architecture.

To qualify for the CISSP exam, candidates must have at least five years of professional work experience in information security.

For those without the required experience, passing the exam will grant them an Associate of (ISC)² designation until they meet the experience requirement.

The Certified Information Security Manager (CISM) certification is tailored for individuals aspiring to manage and oversee cybersecurity programs.

CISM focuses on areas such as risk management, incident response, and governance.

Candidates can prepare for the CISM exam by studying the official CISM Review Manual and using practice questions and answers.

Another widely recognized certification is the Certified Information Systems Auditor (CISA), which emphasizes auditing, control, and assurance.

CISA certification is ideal for individuals who want to specialize in auditing information systems and ensuring their security and compliance.

To earn CISA certification, candidates must pass the CISA exam and meet specific work experience requirements.

The Certified Cloud Security Professional (CCSP) certification is designed for professionals working with cloud technologies.

It covers cloud security concepts, cloud architecture, and risk management in cloud environments.

CCSP certification is valuable for those involved in securing cloud-based solutions and services.

To prepare for the CCSP exam, candidates can use official study materials and practice exams.

These are just a few examples of the many cybersecurity certifications available.

The right certification for an individual depends on their career goals, experience level, and areas of interest within cybersecurity.

It's essential to research and select certifications that align with one's desired career path.

In addition to certifications, education paths play a significant role in cybersecurity career development.

Many universities and colleges offer cybersecurity degree programs at the undergraduate and graduate levels.

A Bachelor of Science in Cybersecurity typically covers a broad range of topics, including network security, cryptography, and cyber law.

For individuals who already have a bachelor's degree in another field, many institutions offer master's programs in cybersecurity.

These programs often provide advanced knowledge and specialized training in areas such as digital forensics and cyber risk management.

Furthermore, online education platforms and Massive Open Online Courses (MOOCs) offer cybersecurity courses and specializations.

These online resources allow individuals to acquire cybersecurity knowledge and skills at their own pace and convenience.

Many of these courses are offered by top universities and institutions, making high-quality education accessible to a global audience.

One popular platform for online cybersecurity courses is Coursera, which offers courses and specializations in collaboration with universities and organizations.

For example, the "Cybersecurity Specialization" offered by the University of Maryland covers topics like software security and risk management.

Another valuable resource is edX, which provides cybersecurity courses from institutions like MIT and Harvard University.

The "Cybersecurity MicroMasters Program" offered by RIT (Rochester Institute of Technology) on edX is a comprehensive option for individuals looking to build expertise in cybersecurity.

Hands-on experience is a crucial aspect of cybersecurity education.

Individuals can gain practical skills by participating in capture the flag (CTF) competitions, where they solve cybersecurity challenges and puzzles.

CTF competitions, often organized by cybersecurity communities and universities, provide opportunities to test and improve one's technical abilities.

There are also cybersecurity labs and virtual environments where individuals can practice their skills in a controlled and safe setting.

One such virtual environment is Metasploitable, which is intentionally vulnerable and used for ethical hacking practice.

To deploy Metasploitable on a Linux system, individuals can use virtualization software like VirtualBox or VMware.

First, they need to download the Metasploitable image and import it into the virtualization software.

Once the virtual machine is running, individuals can practice various penetration testing techniques on it.

Another hands-on approach is setting up a home lab with multiple virtual machines to simulate real-world network configurations and security scenarios.

By experimenting with different security tools and configurations, individuals can gain valuable experience and understanding.

Cybersecurity education and certification paths are not limited to technical roles.

Many organizations and government agencies seek cybersecurity professionals for policy development, compliance, and risk management.

These roles often require a strong understanding of cybersecurity principles and regulations.

To excel in these positions, individuals can pursue certifications such as Certified Information Security Manager (CISM) or

Certified Information Systems Auditor (CISA), as mentioned earlier.

In summary, certifications and education paths are essential components of a successful career in cybersecurity.

Certifications validate expertise in specific areas of cybersecurity, while education paths provide comprehensive knowledge and skills.

The right combination of certifications and education can open doors to various career opportunities in this dynamic and critical field.

Whether aspiring to be a cybersecurity analyst, penetration tester, security consultant, or manager, individuals can tailor their certification and education choices to align with their career goals and interests.

By continually learning and staying updated with industry trends, cybersecurity professionals can thrive in a field that plays a vital role in safeguarding digital assets and privacy in today's interconnected world.

BOOK 2
TROJAN EXPOSED
MASTERING ADVANCED THREAT DETECTION

ROB BOTWRIGHT

Chapter 1: The Evolution of Cyber Threats

The historical cyber threat landscape provides valuable insights into the evolution of cybersecurity challenges over time.

To understand the current state of cybersecurity and anticipate future threats, it is essential to examine the past.

In the early days of computing, cyber threats were relatively limited, with most systems isolated and not interconnected.

As technology advanced and the internet became pervasive, new opportunities for cyberattacks emerged.

One of the earliest and most well-known cyber threats was the computer virus.

Computer viruses are malicious programs designed to replicate and spread from one computer to another, often causing damage or stealing data.

The first widely recognized computer virus, known as the "Creeper" virus, was created in the early 1970s and spread on ARPANET, a precursor to the internet.

The Creeper virus displayed a message on infected computers, stating, "I'm the creeper, catch me if you can!"

To remove the Creeper virus, researchers developed the first antivirus program called "Reaper."

The concept of antivirus software emerged as a response to these early threats.

Over the years, cyber threats continued to evolve, leading to the development of various malware types, including worms, Trojans, and spyware.

Worms, such as the Morris Worm in 1988, were self-replicating programs that spread across networks, causing widespread disruptions.

The Morris Worm, created by Robert Tappan Morris, infected thousands of computers and highlighted the need for better network security.

Trojan horses, named after the ancient Greek story of the wooden horse used to infiltrate Troy, are deceptive programs that appear harmless but contain hidden malicious code.

Spyware, on the other hand, silently collects user information without their knowledge or consent.

The early 2000s saw the emergence of more sophisticated cyber threats, including the infamous "ILOVEYOU" worm in 2000.

The ILOVEYOU worm spread rapidly via email, causing extensive damage by overwriting files and stealing user passwords.

This incident underscored the vulnerabilities of email systems and the need for improved email security.

As the internet continued to grow, cybercriminals began targeting e-commerce websites and online financial transactions.

Phishing attacks became prevalent, with cybercriminals posing as legitimate entities to trick users into disclosing sensitive information.

Phishing emails often contained links to fraudulent websites that mimicked trusted organizations.

To protect against phishing, organizations and web browsers implemented security measures such as email filtering and website identity verification.

While cyber threats were primarily driven by individual hackers in the early days, the landscape changed with the emergence of organized cybercrime groups and nation-state actors.

Organized cybercrime groups, often operating for financial gain, became more sophisticated in their tactics and techniques.

They targeted individuals, businesses, and financial institutions, causing substantial financial losses.

Nation-state actors, including government-sponsored hackers, engaged in cyber espionage and cyber warfare, targeting other countries' critical infrastructure and military systems.

One notable example was the Stuxnet worm, discovered in 2010, which targeted Iran's nuclear program.

Stuxnet demonstrated the potential for cyberattacks to disrupt physical infrastructure and highlighted the need for robust cybersecurity measures in critical sectors.

As technology continued to advance, the Internet of Things (IoT) brought new challenges to the cyber threat landscape.

IoT devices, ranging from smart home appliances to industrial sensors, often lacked security features, making them vulnerable to exploitation.

Cybercriminals capitalized on these vulnerabilities to launch attacks, such as the Mirai botnet in 2016, which targeted IoT devices to launch massive Distributed Denial of Service (DDoS) attacks.

The Mirai botnet infected hundreds of thousands of IoT devices, highlighting the importance of securing IoT ecosystems.

Another significant development in the historical cyber threat landscape was the rise of ransomware attacks.

Ransomware is malicious software that encrypts a victim's data and demands a ransom in exchange for the decryption key.

The WannaCry ransomware attack in 2017 garnered worldwide attention as it spread rapidly, affecting organizations and critical infrastructure.

WannaCry exploited a vulnerability in Microsoft Windows, emphasizing the importance of timely patching and vulnerability management.

In response to the increasing frequency and impact of cyber threats, governments and international organizations began to take cybersecurity more seriously.

Cybersecurity frameworks and regulations were introduced to enhance the resilience of critical infrastructure and protect sensitive data.

For instance, the European Union's General Data Protection Regulation (GDPR) imposed strict data protection requirements on organizations handling personal data.

The historical cyber threat landscape also witnessed the emergence of advanced persistent threats (APTs).

APTs are long-term cyber espionage campaigns conducted by well-funded and organized adversaries.

These campaigns often target governments, corporations, and critical infrastructure with the aim of stealing sensitive information or disrupting operations.

Notable APT groups, such as APT28 (Fancy Bear) and APT29 (Cozy Bear), have been linked to nation-state actors.

To defend against APTs, organizations adopted advanced security measures, including threat intelligence sharing and continuous monitoring.

The development of artificial intelligence (AI) and machine learning (ML) introduced new dynamics to the cyber threat landscape.

While AI and ML technologies can enhance cybersecurity by automating threat detection and response, they can also be used by cybercriminals to create more sophisticated and adaptive attacks.

This cat-and-mouse game between cybersecurity professionals and threat actors continues to evolve.

The historical cyber threat landscape serves as a reminder that cybersecurity is an ongoing battle.

It requires continuous innovation, collaboration, and vigilance to stay ahead of evolving threats.

As technology continues to advance with trends like cloud computing, 5G connectivity, and quantum computing, the future of the cyber threat landscape remains uncertain.

However, by learning from the past and staying informed about emerging threats, individuals and organizations can better prepare for the cybersecurity challenges of tomorrow.

Modern trends in cyberattacks reveal an ever-evolving landscape of threats and techniques that pose significant challenges to cybersecurity professionals and organizations.

One prominent trend is the rise of ransomware attacks, where cybercriminals encrypt a victim's data and demand a ransom for its release.

Ransomware has become increasingly sophisticated, with attackers targeting critical infrastructure, healthcare systems, and municipalities.

To mitigate the risk of ransomware, organizations must implement robust backup and recovery strategies and regularly update security measures.

Another concerning trend is the growth of supply chain attacks, where attackers compromise a trusted vendor or supplier to gain access to a target organization's network.

The SolarWinds incident in 2020 exemplified the potential impact of supply chain attacks on government agencies and businesses.

To defend against supply chain attacks, organizations should assess third-party security practices and conduct thorough risk assessments.

Credential stuffing attacks have also gained prominence, where attackers use stolen username and password combinations to gain unauthorized access to multiple accounts.

These attacks exploit individuals who reuse passwords across multiple platforms.

To counter credential stuffing, users should employ strong, unique passwords for each account, and organizations can implement multi-factor authentication (MFA) to enhance security.

Social engineering attacks, including phishing and spear-phishing, remain prevalent and effective tactics for cybercriminals.

Phishing attacks involve deceptive emails or messages that trick recipients into revealing sensitive information or clicking on malicious links.

Spear-phishing targets specific individuals within an organization, often with highly personalized messages.

User awareness training and email filtering solutions are critical to preventing social engineering attacks.

One emerging trend in cyberattacks is the targeting of remote work environments, driven by the global shift to remote work during the COVID-19 pandemic.

Attackers exploit vulnerabilities in remote access solutions and home networks to gain unauthorized access to corporate systems.

Organizations must secure remote work environments with updated software, VPNs, and endpoint security solutions.

Advanced Persistent Threat (APT) groups, often attributed to nation-state actors, continue to conduct long-term cyber espionage campaigns targeting governments and industries.

These adversaries employ sophisticated techniques and zero-day vulnerabilities to maintain persistent access.

To counter APTs, organizations need robust threat detection, incident response, and threat intelligence capabilities.

Cryptocurrency-related cybercrimes, such as cryptojacking and ransomware payments in cryptocurrency, have surged as cryptocurrencies gained popularity.

Cryptojacking involves illicitly using victims' computing resources to mine cryptocurrencies.

Organizations must monitor for signs of cryptojacking and establish policies for dealing with ransomware payment requests.

The use of artificial intelligence (AI) and machine learning (ML) by both cyber attackers and defenders represents a growing trend.

Attackers leverage AI to automate attacks and evade traditional security measures, while defenders use AI and ML to detect and respond to threats.

As AI and ML adoption increases, organizations need to invest in AI-driven cybersecurity solutions to keep pace with evolving threats.

Another concerning development is the exploitation of vulnerabilities in Internet of Things (IoT) devices, as the number of connected devices continues to grow.

Attackers target unpatched or poorly secured IoT devices to gain a foothold in a network.

Organizations must implement strong IoT security measures, including firmware updates and network segmentation.

Fileless malware attacks have gained popularity due to their stealthy nature.

Fileless malware operates in memory, making it challenging to detect with traditional antivirus software.

Defenders must rely on behavior-based analysis and endpoint detection and response (EDR) solutions to identify and block fileless malware.

The growing trend of disinformation campaigns and cyber influence operations poses a unique challenge.

State-sponsored actors and threat groups use social media platforms and fake news to manipulate public opinion and spread false information.

Addressing this trend requires a combination of cybersecurity measures and media literacy efforts.

While not new, zero-day vulnerabilities continue to be a lucrative asset for attackers.

Zero-days are software vulnerabilities that are unknown to the vendor and lack available patches.

Attackers use zero-days to conduct targeted attacks, emphasizing the importance of proactive vulnerability management and threat hunting.

The increase in attacks targeting cloud services and cloud-based infrastructure reflects the broader adoption of cloud computing.

Attackers exploit misconfigured cloud resources, insecure APIs, and weak access controls.

Organizations must implement proper cloud security measures, including regular security assessments and configuration monitoring.

Finally, the use of automation and orchestration in cyberattacks enables attackers to scale their operations efficiently.

Automated attacks can exploit vulnerabilities and launch attacks at a speed that overwhelms traditional defenses.

Defenders need to deploy automated threat detection and response solutions to counter these attacks effectively.

In summary, modern trends in cyberattacks demonstrate the ongoing evolution of cyber threats, driven by technology advancements and changing attack tactics.

Organizations and cybersecurity professionals must remain vigilant, adapt to these trends, and continually enhance their cybersecurity strategies and tools to protect against emerging threats.

As the digital landscape continues to evolve, proactive cybersecurity measures and threat intelligence will play crucial roles in defending against cyberattacks.

Chapter 2: Advanced Trojan Variants and Techniques

The evolution and mutation of Trojans represent a constant challenge in the ever-changing landscape of cybersecurity.

Trojans, named after the ancient Greek tale of the Trojan Horse, are deceptive malware that appear benign but contain hidden malicious code.

They have been a staple of cyberattacks since the early days of computing.

The primary goal of a Trojan is to infiltrate a victim's system without detection, providing attackers with unauthorized access and control.

Early Trojans were relatively simple, often limited to basic functions like data theft or remote access.

As the field of cybersecurity advanced, so did the sophistication of Trojans.

They evolved to become more complex, multifunctional, and evasive.

One notable milestone in Trojan evolution was the emergence of remote access Trojans (RATs).

RATs allowed attackers to gain full control over an infected system, enabling activities such as keystroke logging, screen capture, and file manipulation.

These capabilities made them particularly effective for cyber espionage and data theft.

To deploy a RAT, attackers often rely on social engineering techniques, phishing emails, or malicious downloads.

The evolution of Trojans also saw the development of specialized variants, tailored to specific objectives.

Banking Trojans, for example, are designed to target online banking systems.

They intercept login credentials and manipulate transactions, allowing attackers to steal funds.

Zeus, also known as Zbot, was one of the earliest and most notorious banking Trojans.

To protect against banking Trojans, users should exercise caution when accessing online banking services and keep their systems and antivirus software up to date.

Another significant development in Trojan evolution was the use of polymorphic and metamorphic techniques.

Polymorphic Trojans change their code structure each time they infect a system, making detection by signature-based antivirus software challenging.

Metamorphic Trojans go a step further by completely rewriting their code while retaining the same functionality.

These techniques allow Trojans to evade traditional antivirus defenses.

To counter polymorphic and metamorphic Trojans, heuristic and behavior-based analysis methods became crucial for threat detection.

One of the most infamous examples of a polymorphic Trojan was Storm Worm, which circulated in 2007.

Its constant mutation made it difficult to eradicate, and it was often distributed via spam emails.

To remove Storm Worm from an infected system, users could employ antivirus software with heuristic detection capabilities.

Another significant advancement in Trojan evolution involved rootkits.

Rootkits are malicious software components that hide the presence of Trojans or other malware on a system by modifying or subverting the operating system.

They provide stealth and persistence, making them challenging to detect and remove.

To detect and remove rootkits, users can employ specialized rootkit detection and removal tools or perform a full system reinstallation.

The emergence of advanced persistent threats (APTs) marked a new phase in Trojan evolution.

APTs are sophisticated and long-term cyber espionage campaigns conducted by well-funded and organized threat actors, often nation-states.

Trojans played a pivotal role in APTs, serving as the initial entry point into target systems.

One infamous APT group, APT28 (also known as Fancy Bear), used Trojans to infiltrate government agencies and organizations worldwide.

To protect against APTs, organizations must implement robust security measures, conduct regular security assessments, and monitor for signs of compromise.

Another aspect of Trojan evolution involved the expansion of targeted attacks against specific industries and sectors.

For example, the healthcare sector became a prime target, with Trojans designed to steal patient data and compromise medical devices.

The NotPetya ransomware attack in 2017, which initially appeared to be a ransomware Trojan, primarily targeted Ukraine's healthcare system but had collateral damage worldwide.

To secure healthcare systems, organizations should implement network segmentation, encryption, and access controls.

Mobile Trojans, or mobile malware, also became a significant threat as smartphones and tablets became ubiquitous.

These Trojans targeted mobile devices, stealing personal information, intercepting communications, and compromising mobile banking apps.

To protect against mobile Trojans, users should download apps only from reputable sources and keep their mobile devices updated with the latest security patches.

One notable mobile Trojan was HummingBad, a sophisticated malware campaign that infected millions of Android devices in 2016.

The Trojan generated revenue for its operators through ad fraud and app installations.

To remove HummingBad from an infected Android device, users could perform a factory reset or use mobile antivirus software.

The evolution of Trojans continued with the development of fileless Trojans.

Fileless Trojans operate in memory, leaving no traditional file traces on the infected system.

They leverage legitimate system tools and processes to carry out malicious activities, making detection and removal challenging.

To counter fileless Trojans, organizations should implement advanced endpoint security solutions that focus on behavior-based analysis.

As the sophistication of Trojans increased, so did the need for threat intelligence sharing and collaborative cybersecurity efforts.

The cybersecurity community relies on information sharing to identify and respond to emerging threats.

Additionally, machine learning and artificial intelligence have become essential tools for detecting Trojans and other advanced malware.

These technologies can analyze vast amounts of data and identify patterns indicative of Trojan activity.

To stay ahead of evolving Trojans, organizations must invest in cutting-edge cybersecurity solutions and prioritize ongoing threat research.

The evolution and mutation of Trojans underscore the need for a multi-layered approach to cybersecurity, including strong perimeter defenses, endpoint security, user education, and threat intelligence sharing.

By staying vigilant and proactive, individuals and organizations can better defend against the ever-changing threat landscape presented by Trojans and their malicious counterparts.

Advanced delivery and evasion techniques represent a crucial aspect of modern cyberattacks, as cybercriminals continually seek ways to bypass security measures and reach their targets undetected.

These techniques encompass a wide range of strategies and tactics designed to deliver malicious payloads and avoid detection by security systems.

One commonly used delivery method is phishing emails, which involve tricking individuals into clicking on malicious links or opening malicious attachments.

Attackers often craft convincing emails that mimic legitimate organizations or use social engineering to manipulate recipients into taking actions that compromise their security.

To deploy phishing emails, attackers can use readily available email spoofing tools or send emails through compromised email accounts to evade detection.

Another delivery technique is the use of exploit kits, which are malicious frameworks that exploit known vulnerabilities in software and deliver malware to vulnerable systems.

Exploit kits are often embedded in compromised websites, and when users visit these sites, the kits scan for vulnerabilities in their browsers or installed plugins.

One well-known exploit kit is the Blackhole exploit kit, which was commonly used to deliver Trojans and ransomware.

To mitigate the risk of exploit kit attacks, users should keep their software and plugins up to date and use security plugins that block malicious content.

Advanced delivery techniques also include the use of watering hole attacks, where attackers compromise websites that are frequently visited by their target audience.

By infecting a trusted site, attackers increase the likelihood of their targets visiting the compromised site and unknowingly downloading malicious payloads.

To deploy a watering hole attack, attackers can exploit vulnerabilities in the site's content management system or inject malicious code into web pages.

To defend against such attacks, website owners must maintain strong security practices and continuously monitor their websites for signs of compromise.

Malvertising, short for malicious advertising, is another delivery method that leverages online advertisements to deliver malware.

Attackers compromise ad networks or place malicious ads on legitimate websites, and when users click on these ads, they are redirected to sites that deliver malware.

To protect against malvertising, users should use ad-blockers and keep their browsers and plugins updated.

Additionally, organizations should implement web filtering and security solutions that block malicious ads.

The use of drive-by downloads is another advanced delivery technique, where attackers automatically download malicious software onto a victim's system without their consent or knowledge.

These downloads occur when a user visits a compromised website that exploits vulnerabilities in the user's browser or plugins.

Drive-by download attacks often deliver Trojans, ransomware, or spyware.

To deploy drive-by download attacks, attackers can use exploit kits or malicious scripts injected into web pages.

To protect against drive-by downloads, users should disable unnecessary plugins, use browser security settings, and employ browser extensions that block malicious scripts.

The use of malicious email attachments is a classic delivery technique that remains effective.

Attackers attach malicious files to emails, often using common file types like Microsoft Word or PDF documents.

When recipients open these attachments, they unwittingly execute the embedded malware.

To defend against malicious email attachments, users should exercise caution when opening attachments, especially if the email is unexpected or from an unknown sender.

Antivirus software and email security filters can also detect and quarantine malicious attachments.

Social engineering tactics play a significant role in advanced delivery techniques.

Attackers use social engineering to manipulate individuals into taking actions that compromise their security.

These tactics can include impersonating trusted entities, creating a sense of urgency, or exploiting emotions like fear or curiosity.

To defend against social engineering, individuals and organizations should educate users about common tactics and encourage a healthy skepticism toward unsolicited requests or communications.

Another delivery method involves using malicious macros in documents.

Attackers embed malicious macros, typically in Microsoft Office documents, which are executed when the document is opened.

These macros can download and execute malware onto the victim's system.

To deploy this technique, attackers can send documents via email or deliver them through malicious websites.

To protect against malicious macros, users should disable macros by default and only enable them for trusted documents.

Additionally, organizations can implement security policies that restrict the use of macros.

Advanced evasion techniques focus on avoiding detection by security systems once a payload is delivered.

One common evasion method is code obfuscation, where attackers intentionally obscure their malware's code to make it more challenging to analyze.

Obfuscated code can make signature-based detection ineffective, as the malware's code appears different each time it is delivered.

To deploy code obfuscation, attackers can use tools that automatically transform their code or manually manipulate it.

To counter code obfuscation, security researchers and organizations rely on behavior-based analysis and heuristic detection methods.

Another evasion technique is the use of encrypted communications to conceal malicious activity.

Attackers can encrypt their communication channels using secure protocols like HTTPS or use encrypted tunnels like Virtual Private Networks (VPNs) to hide their actions.

These encrypted communications make it difficult for security systems to inspect network traffic for signs of malicious behavior.

To detect malicious activity in encrypted traffic, organizations can employ security solutions that perform deep packet inspection and analyze network behavior.

To further evade detection, attackers can employ polymorphic malware, which continually changes its code to create unique variants of the same malware family.

Polymorphic malware can bypass signature-based detection and make it challenging for security systems to identify recurring patterns.

To deploy polymorphic malware, attackers can use code generators that automatically generate new variants with each delivery.

To detect polymorphic malware, security solutions often rely on behavioral analysis and heuristics to identify malicious behavior.

To defend against advanced delivery and evasion techniques, organizations must adopt a multi-layered security approach that includes proactive measures such as user education, patch management, and the use of advanced threat detection and prevention solutions.

Additionally, organizations should stay informed about the latest attack techniques and continually update their security strategies to adapt to evolving threats.

Chapter 3: Deep Dive into Trojan Payloads and Exploits

The anatomy of Trojan payloads reveals the inner workings of these malicious components that lie at the heart of Trojan attacks.

A Trojan payload is the part of the malware that carries out the specific malicious actions intended by the attacker.

Understanding how Trojan payloads function is essential for cybersecurity professionals and organizations seeking to defend against these threats.

Trojan payloads come in various forms, depending on the attacker's objectives.

One common type of payload is a backdoor, which provides unauthorized access to an infected system.

A backdoor allows attackers to control the compromised system remotely, execute commands, and exfiltrate data.

To deploy a backdoor payload, attackers often exploit vulnerabilities in the target system or use social engineering to trick users into executing the Trojan.

For example, an attacker might send a malicious email attachment that, when opened, installs a backdoor on the victim's computer.

To protect against backdoor payloads, organizations must maintain strong access controls and regularly update software to patch known vulnerabilities.

Another type of payload is a keylogger, which records keystrokes made by a user.

Keyloggers are often used to steal sensitive information such as login credentials, credit card numbers, or other confidential data.

To deploy a keylogger payload, attackers may bundle it with other software or use drive-by download techniques to silently infect a victim's system.

To detect and remove keyloggers, users can employ antivirus software and regularly scan their systems for malware.

Some payloads are designed for financial gain, such as banking Trojans.

These Trojans target online banking systems and attempt to steal login credentials, manipulate transactions, or siphon funds from victims' accounts.

To deploy a banking Trojan payload, attackers may use phishing emails or malicious attachments to infect a user's device.

To protect against banking Trojans, users should be cautious when accessing online banking services and use two-factor authentication (2FA) where available.

Ransomware payloads have gained notoriety in recent years, encrypting a victim's files and demanding a ransom for the decryption key.

Ransomware attacks often lead to data loss and financial harm to victims.

To deploy a ransomware payload, attackers typically use malicious email attachments, exploit vulnerabilities, or deliver payloads via malicious websites.

To defend against ransomware, organizations should maintain robust backup and recovery solutions and regularly educate users about the risks of clicking on suspicious links or opening unknown attachments.

Payloads can also be designed for espionage, where the objective is to steal sensitive information or monitor a victim's activities.

These espionage payloads may include capabilities for capturing screenshots, recording audio, or exfiltrating documents.

To deploy espionage payloads, attackers may use sophisticated social engineering tactics or target specific individuals or organizations.

To defend against espionage payloads, organizations should implement strong network monitoring and endpoint security solutions.

Some Trojan payloads are crafted for distributed denial-of-service (DDoS) attacks.

These payloads allow an attacker to control a network of compromised devices, known as a botnet, to flood a target's systems with traffic, overwhelming them and causing disruption.

To deploy DDoS payloads, attackers often compromise a large number of devices, such as IoT devices, and coordinate them to launch an attack.

To defend against DDoS attacks, organizations can employ traffic filtering, load balancing, and content delivery networks (CDNs).

Payloads can also include rootkit functionality, allowing attackers to maintain persistent access and control over an infected system.

Rootkits are difficult to detect and remove, making them a valuable tool for attackers.

To deploy a rootkit payload, attackers typically exploit vulnerabilities or use social engineering techniques to gain access to a target system.

To protect against rootkits, organizations should implement strong access controls, regularly update software, and use security solutions that detect and remove rootkit components.

Some payloads are designed to deliver spam or propagate further malware infections.

These payloads may use infected systems to send spam emails or scan for other vulnerable devices to infect.

To deploy these payloads, attackers often use exploit kits, malicious attachments, or compromised websites.

To defend against spam and malware propagation, organizations should use email filtering solutions and network security measures.

Advanced Trojan payloads often employ evasion techniques to avoid detection by security software and analysis tools.

One common evasion technique is code obfuscation, where attackers intentionally obscure their payload's code to make it more difficult to analyze.

Code obfuscation can thwart signature-based detection methods.

To defend against obfuscated payloads, security researchers and organizations rely on behavior-based analysis and heuristics.

Another evasion technique is encryption, where the payload's code or communication channels are encrypted to hide malicious activity.

This can make it challenging for security systems to inspect network traffic or analyze the payload.

To detect malicious activity in encrypted traffic, organizations should use security solutions that perform deep packet inspection and analyze network behavior.

Polymorphic payloads continually change their code structure, creating unique variants of the same malware family with each delivery.

This dynamic behavior makes it difficult for signature-based detection methods to identify recurring patterns.

To detect polymorphic payloads, security solutions often rely on behavioral analysis and heuristics to identify malicious behavior.

Ultimately, understanding the anatomy of Trojan payloads is crucial for developing effective defense strategies against these malicious components.

Organizations must employ a multi-layered approach to cybersecurity that includes user education, regular software updates, strong access controls, and advanced threat detection solutions.

By staying informed about the latest Trojan payload techniques and continuously adapting their security measures, individuals and organizations can better defend against the evolving threat landscape.

Zero-day exploits and advanced attack vectors represent some of the most potent and elusive threats in the world of cybersecurity.

A zero-day exploit is a cyberattack that targets a vulnerability in software or hardware before the vendor has had a chance to develop and release a patch or fix for it.

These exploits are called "zero-day" because they occur on the very day the vulnerability is discovered, leaving zero days for the vendor to address the issue.

Zero-day vulnerabilities are highly sought after by cybercriminals and state-sponsored hacking groups, as they provide a unique opportunity to compromise systems without the risk of being detected and patched.

To deploy a zero-day exploit, attackers typically use a combination of reverse engineering, vulnerability scanning, and in-depth knowledge of the targeted software.

One well-known example of a zero-day exploit is the Stuxnet worm, which targeted industrial control systems and exploited multiple zero-day vulnerabilities.

Stuxnet's advanced attack vectors and use of zero-days made it one of the most sophisticated and destructive malware in history.

To defend against zero-day exploits, organizations should prioritize vulnerability management, implement intrusion detection systems, and employ network segmentation to limit the potential impact of a successful attack.

Advanced attack vectors are the methods and techniques used by cyber attackers to infiltrate systems and networks, often bypassing traditional security measures.

These vectors go beyond typical attack methods and leverage a combination of tactics to achieve their objectives.

One advanced attack vector is the use of supply chain attacks, where attackers compromise a trusted vendor or supplier to gain access to a target organization's network.

Supply chain attacks can be challenging to detect, as attackers exploit the trust that organizations have in their suppliers.

To defend against supply chain attacks, organizations should conduct thorough risk assessments of their suppliers and implement strict security controls.

Another advanced attack vector involves zero-day exploits, which we previously discussed.

Zero-days are highly effective attack vectors, as they target vulnerabilities that are unknown to the vendor and, therefore, lack available patches.

To protect against zero-day exploits, organizations should employ proactive security measures, such as threat intelligence sharing and the use of behavior-based anomaly detection systems.

Social engineering is a prevalent advanced attack vector, encompassing tactics like phishing, spear-phishing, and pretexting.

These techniques manipulate human psychology to trick individuals into divulging sensitive information or performing actions that compromise security.

To deploy social engineering attacks, attackers craft convincing emails or messages that appear legitimate.

To defend against social engineering, organizations should provide user awareness training and implement email filtering solutions that detect and quarantine phishing emails.

Another advanced attack vector is the use of fileless malware, which operates in memory and leaves no traditional file traces on the infected system.

Fileless malware leverages legitimate system tools and processes to carry out malicious activities, making detection and removal challenging.

To deploy fileless malware, attackers may use malicious scripts or take advantage of vulnerabilities in the operating system.

To detect and respond to fileless malware, organizations should deploy endpoint detection and response (EDR) solutions that focus on behavior-based analysis.

Watering hole attacks involve compromising websites that are frequently visited by the target audience, increasing the likelihood of victims visiting the compromised site and unknowingly downloading malicious payloads.

To deploy a watering hole attack, attackers exploit vulnerabilities in the site's content management system or inject malicious code into web pages.

To defend against watering hole attacks, website owners should maintain strong security practices and monitor their sites for signs of compromise.

Man-in-the-middle (MitM) attacks are another advanced attack vector, where an attacker intercepts communications between two parties without their knowledge.

MitM attackers can eavesdrop on conversations, steal data, or manipulate information exchanged between the parties.

To deploy a MitM attack, attackers may exploit vulnerabilities in network protocols or compromise network devices.

To protect against MitM attacks, organizations should use encryption protocols and regularly update network equipment.

Advanced attack vectors also include physical attacks on hardware and infrastructure.

For example, attackers may gain physical access to a data center or server room to compromise hardware or install malicious devices.

To defend against physical attacks, organizations should implement strong access controls, surveillance, and security protocols for their physical facilities.

Additionally, organizations should be aware of insider threats, as employees or insiders with privileged access can be used as advanced attack vectors.

Insiders may intentionally or unintentionally compromise security, making it essential for organizations to implement strict access controls and monitoring mechanisms.

Lastly, advanced attack vectors may involve leveraging artificial intelligence (AI) and machine learning (ML) technologies.

Attackers can use AI and ML to automate attacks, evade detection, and scale their operations.

To defend against AI-driven attacks, organizations must invest in AI-powered cybersecurity solutions that can detect and respond to evolving threats.

In summary, zero-day exploits and advanced attack vectors pose significant challenges to cybersecurity.

These threats are continuously evolving, making it crucial for organizations to adopt a proactive and multi-layered security approach.

This approach should include regular vulnerability assessments, user education, threat intelligence sharing, and the use of advanced security solutions.

By staying vigilant and adapting to the changing threat landscape, organizations can better defend against these potent and elusive cyber threats.

Chapter 4: Advanced Threat Intelligence and Analysis

Threat intelligence gathering is a critical component of modern cybersecurity, providing organizations with valuable insights into emerging threats and vulnerabilities.

Effective threat intelligence enables organizations to proactively defend against cyberattacks and make informed decisions about their security posture.

The process of threat intelligence gathering begins with the collection of data from various sources, both internal and external.

External sources include open-source information, security research reports, and threat feeds from cybersecurity vendors.

Internal sources consist of data generated within an organization's network and systems, such as logs, incident reports, and network traffic analysis.

To gather threat intelligence from external sources, cybersecurity professionals often use specialized tools and platforms that aggregate and analyze data from multiple feeds.

One such tool is Threat Intelligence Platforms (TIPs), which provide a centralized hub for collecting, correlating, and analyzing threat data.

To deploy a TIP, organizations can follow these steps:

Select a reputable Threat Intelligence Platform that aligns with their needs and budget.

Install and configure the TIP according to the vendor's guidelines.

Integrate the TIP with existing security systems and data sources, such as SIEM (Security Information and Event Management) solutions.

Set up data feeds from external threat intelligence providers and customize the platform's settings.

Define workflows and automation rules to prioritize and act on incoming threat intelligence.

Train cybersecurity personnel to effectively use the TIP for threat detection and response.

Open-source threat intelligence feeds, like the ones provided by organizations such as the Cyber Threat Intelligence Sharing Center (CTIIC) or the Multi-State Information Sharing and Analysis Center (MS-ISAC), are valuable sources for collecting indicators of compromise (IoCs) and other threat data.

Cybersecurity professionals can use command-line tools like "curl" or "wget" to access and retrieve data from these feeds.

For instance, to fetch threat intelligence data from a CTIIC feed, one can use the following command:

shellCopy code

```
curl -O https://example.com/threat-feed.json
```

Once data is collected, it undergoes analysis to identify patterns, trends, and potential threats.

Cybersecurity analysts use various techniques, including data mining, statistical analysis, and machine learning, to extract meaningful insights from the collected information.

Threat intelligence analysts often utilize command-line tools and scripts to process and analyze large datasets efficiently.

For example, they may use the "grep" command to search for specific keywords or indicators in log files:

shellCopy code

```
grep "malicious IP" access.log
```

To enrich threat intelligence data, organizations can employ open-source and commercial threat intelligence feeds that provide additional context, such as threat actor profiles, malware descriptions, and attack techniques.

These feeds can be integrated into the organization's security infrastructure using APIs or standardized formats like STIX/TAXII (Structured Threat Information eXpression / Trusted Automated Exchange of Indicator Information).

Once threat intelligence has been gathered and analyzed, organizations can use it to enhance their security posture in several ways.

One common use case is the creation of threat intelligence feeds for security tools like intrusion detection systems (IDS) and firewalls.

These feeds contain IoCs and rules that enable security solutions to automatically detect and block known threats.

To deploy threat intelligence feeds in an IDS, organizations can follow these steps:

Access the IDS management console.

Import the threat intelligence feed in a compatible format (e.g., Snort rules, Suricata rules, or YARA rules).

Configure the IDS to regularly update the feed to stay current with emerging threats.

Monitor the IDS alerts and investigate any triggered by the newly added threat intelligence rules.

Fine-tune the rules and alerts as needed to reduce false positives.

Another way organizations can leverage threat intelligence is by integrating it into their Security Information and Event Management (SIEM) systems.

SIEM solutions provide centralized log and event management, making them an ideal platform for correlating threat intelligence data with real-time security events.

To integrate threat intelligence into a SIEM, organizations can use the SIEM vendor's documentation and guidelines.

Typically, it involves configuring data sources, creating custom parsers or connectors, and setting up correlation rules to detect and respond to threats.

Additionally, threat intelligence can inform incident response strategies and help organizations prioritize their response efforts.

When a security incident occurs, threat intelligence analysts can quickly determine whether the incident aligns with known threat actor behavior or tactics.

They can use threat intelligence to identify the likely source of the attack, its objectives, and the potential impact on the organization.

This information enables incident responders to tailor their actions effectively and mitigate the threat.

To operationalize threat intelligence in incident response, organizations can establish incident response playbooks and procedures that incorporate threat intelligence data.

These playbooks should outline how to investigate and respond to different types of threats based on the available intelligence.

Moreover, threat intelligence can aid in threat hunting, a proactive approach to cybersecurity where analysts actively seek out hidden threats within an organization's environment.

Threat hunters use threat intelligence to guide their investigations, focusing on areas of the network or specific behaviors that align with known threat indicators.

To conduct threat hunting, organizations can deploy skilled analysts equipped with the necessary tools and access to threat intelligence feeds.

The process often involves command-line tools, network monitoring, and analysis of logs and endpoints.

In summary, threat intelligence gathering is a crucial practice in modern cybersecurity.

Organizations can use various sources and tools to collect, analyze, and operationalize threat intelligence to strengthen their security posture.

By integrating threat intelligence into their security infrastructure, organizations can proactively defend against cyber threats and respond effectively when incidents occur.

Advanced threat analysis techniques are essential for

identifying and mitigating sophisticated cyber threats that pose significant risks to organizations and individuals.

These techniques go beyond basic security measures and delve into the intricacies of cyberattacks to understand their tactics, techniques, and procedures (TTPs).

One fundamental aspect of advanced threat analysis is malware analysis, which involves dissecting malicious software to uncover its functionality and purpose.

To perform malware analysis, security analysts often use specialized tools and sandboxes.

For instance, the "Cuckoo Sandbox" is a widely used open-source platform that automates the analysis of suspicious files and documents.

To analyze a suspicious file with Cuckoo Sandbox, you can execute the following command:

shellCopy code

```
cuckoo submit suspicious_file.exe
```

Advanced threat analysts also use reverse engineering techniques to dissect malware and understand its inner workings.

Reverse engineering involves examining the binary code of a program to determine its functionality.

Tools like "IDA Pro" and "Ghidra" are commonly used for reverse engineering tasks.

For example, to open a binary file for analysis with Ghidra, you can run the following command:

shellCopy code

```
ghidraRun /path/to/binary/file
```

Another crucial aspect of advanced threat analysis is network traffic analysis.

This technique involves monitoring network traffic to detect suspicious or malicious activities.

Network traffic analysis tools like "Wireshark" allow analysts to capture and analyze packets to identify potential threats.

To capture network traffic using Wireshark, you can run the following command:

shellCopy code

```
wireshark
```

In addition to analyzing individual pieces of malware or network traffic, advanced threat analysis also focuses on understanding the broader threat landscape.

This includes tracking threat actors, their tactics, and their motivations.

Threat intelligence feeds and platforms play a vital role in gathering information about emerging threats and the activities of threat actors.

Cybersecurity professionals can use threat intelligence feeds to enrich their understanding of specific threats and make informed decisions about threat mitigation.

To integrate threat intelligence feeds into their security infrastructure, organizations often use platforms like "MISP" (Malware Information Sharing Platform & Threat Sharing) or "STIX/TAXII" (Structured Threat Information eXpression / Trusted Automated Exchange of Indicator Information) standards.

For instance, to import threat intelligence data into a MISP instance, you can use the following command:

shellCopy code

```
misp-galaxy -e event import /path/to/threat_intelligence.json
```

Behavioral analysis is another advanced threat analysis technique that focuses on understanding how malware or attackers behave within a network or system.

This technique involves monitoring the behavior of software or users and looking for deviations from expected norms.

Behavioral analysis often requires the use of machine learning algorithms and anomaly detection systems to identify suspicious activities.

To deploy behavioral analysis, organizations can utilize endpoint detection and response (EDR) solutions that continuously monitor endpoints for abnormal behavior.

Memory analysis is a critical aspect of advanced threat analysis, particularly when dealing with advanced and evasive malware.

Memory analysis involves examining the contents of a computer's volatile memory, such as RAM, to identify running processes, hidden processes, and other indicators of compromise.

Tools like "Volatility" are commonly used for memory analysis.

To analyze memory dumps with Volatility, you can run commands such as:

```shell
Copy code
volatility -f memory_dump.raw imageinfo
```

```shell
Copy code
volatility -f memory_dump.raw pslist
```

Advanced threat analysis also encompasses threat hunting, which is a proactive approach to identifying hidden threats within an organization's network.

Threat hunters use various techniques, including behavioral analysis and network traffic analysis, to search for signs of compromise.

They often rely on threat intelligence and indicators of compromise (IoCs) to guide their investigations.

To conduct threat hunting, organizations typically employ skilled threat hunters equipped with the necessary tools and access to threat intelligence feeds.

Incident response is a critical component of advanced threat analysis, as it involves taking immediate action to contain and mitigate cyber threats.

Effective incident response requires well-defined processes and procedures, including the use of playbooks that outline steps for different types of incidents.

Incident response teams may also use forensic analysis techniques to gather evidence and determine the scope and impact of an incident.

Forensic analysis involves preserving and analyzing digital evidence, such as log files, system snapshots, and memory dumps.

Digital forensics tools like "Autopsy" and "Sleuth Kit" are commonly used for this purpose.

To analyze a disk image with Autopsy, you can follow a series of commands:

shellCopy code

```
autopsy
```

arduinoCopy code

Choose "New Case" and specify case details.

arduinoCopy code

Add the disk image to the case.

sqlCopy code

Conduct file system and keyword searches within the case.

Copy code

Examine and analyze the results.

In summary, advanced threat analysis techniques are crucial for staying ahead of sophisticated cyber threats.

These techniques encompass malware analysis, network traffic analysis, reverse engineering, threat intelligence, behavioral analysis, memory analysis, threat hunting, and incident response.

By mastering these techniques and employing the appropriate tools and methodologies, cybersecurity professionals can effectively detect, analyze, and mitigate advanced threats, safeguarding their organizations and systems against cyberattacks.

Chapter 5: Network Forensics and Traffic Analysis

Network packet analysis is a crucial skill for cybersecurity professionals, allowing them to inspect and interpret the traffic traversing a network.

This technique involves capturing, examining, and dissecting individual data packets to gain insights into network activity.

To perform network packet analysis, professionals rely on specialized tools such as Wireshark, tcpdump, or tshark.

For example, to capture network packets using tcpdump, one can execute the following command:

shellCopy code

```
tcpdump -i eth0 -w capture.pcap
```

The captured packets are saved in a file called "capture.pcap" for later analysis.

Network packet analysis can serve various purposes, including network troubleshooting, security monitoring, and forensic investigations.

One primary use case is troubleshooting network performance issues.

By examining packet captures, analysts can identify network latency, packet loss, and other anomalies that may affect network performance.

For security monitoring, packet analysis helps detect suspicious or malicious activity on the network.

Analysts look for indicators of compromise (IoCs), unusual traffic patterns, and known attack signatures within the packet data.

Network packet analysis is instrumental in identifying and responding to security incidents.

Forensic investigations often involve analyzing packet captures to reconstruct network activity during a specific timeframe.

Analysts may use these captures to determine the source of a security breach or gather evidence for legal cases.

To analyze network packet data effectively, professionals need to understand the structure of network packets, including headers and payloads.

Network packets typically consist of a header section that contains control information and a payload section that carries the actual data.

Headers contain information such as source and destination IP addresses, port numbers, sequence numbers, and flags.

Analyzing headers provides insights into the source and nature of network traffic.

For instance, by examining the source and destination IP addresses, analysts can determine the communication path and identify potential anomalies.

To delve deeper into packet analysis, professionals should understand common network protocols, such as TCP (Transmission Control Protocol), UDP (User Datagram Protocol), and ICMP (Internet Control Message Protocol).

Each protocol has its own header format and behavior, and experts must recognize the specific fields within these headers for effective analysis.

For instance, TCP packets contain fields like sequence and acknowledgment numbers, which help establish reliable connections and manage data transmission.

UDP packets, on the other hand, lack the reliability mechanisms found in TCP, making them suitable for applications where speed is more critical than data integrity.

ICMP packets are primarily used for network management and troubleshooting, including tasks like ping and traceroute.

To interpret network packets accurately, analysts often use display filters in packet analysis tools to narrow down the data displayed.

For example, in Wireshark, analysts can use display filters to focus on packets that match specific criteria, such as source IP address, destination port, or protocol type.

By applying filters, analysts can isolate relevant packets and reduce the volume of data to review.

Analyzing packet payloads is another critical aspect of network packet analysis, as it can reveal the actual content of network communications.

However, inspecting payload data requires caution, as it may contain sensitive information.

In security-related packet analysis, professionals often look for patterns or signatures of known malware, exploits, or command and control traffic within payload data.

For example, they may search for specific strings or hex values associated with known threats.

To extract payload data from captured packets, analysts can use tools like Wireshark or tcpdump.

Wireshark provides a user-friendly interface for viewing and dissecting packet payloads, while tcpdump allows for command-line extraction.

To extract payload data using tcpdump, one can use a command like the following:

shellCopy code

```
tcpdump -n -A -r capture.pcap | grep "pattern"
```

This command reads the captured packets from the "capture.pcap" file, displays payload data using the "-A" option, and searches for a specific pattern using "grep."

In addition to payload analysis, network packet analysis often involves time-based analysis to understand the sequence and timing of network events.

Professionals may use features like time stamps in packet captures to correlate network activities and identify patterns.

By analyzing the timing of network events, analysts can identify abnormal behavior or coordinated attacks.

Beyond manual analysis, professionals can employ automated tools and techniques for more efficient and comprehensive packet analysis.

These tools often include intrusion detection systems (IDS), intrusion prevention systems (IPS), and network security monitoring (NSM) platforms.

IDS and IPS solutions use predefined rules and signatures to automatically detect and respond to network threats in real-time.

They analyze incoming packets, compare them against known attack patterns, and take action when a match is found.

Network security monitoring platforms provide a centralized view of network activity and often include features for packet capture, storage, and analysis.

These platforms enable security teams to conduct retrospective analysis by reviewing historical packet data.

In summary, network packet analysis is a fundamental skill for cybersecurity professionals tasked with monitoring, troubleshooting, and securing network environments.

By understanding the structure of network packets, recognizing common protocols, and employing effective analysis techniques and tools, experts can uncover valuable insights into network behavior, detect security threats, and respond to incidents effectively.

Identifying anomalies in network traffic is a critical aspect of network security, as it helps organizations detect potential threats and abnormal behavior within their network environments.

Anomalies are deviations from established patterns or baselines in network traffic, and they can be indicative of various security issues, including cyberattacks and insider threats.

To effectively identify anomalies in network traffic, organizations rely on a combination of tools, techniques, and best practices.

One common technique used for anomaly detection is statistical analysis, which involves monitoring various network parameters and identifying deviations from expected values.

For instance, network administrators can use the "netstat" command-line tool to display network statistics and connections on a Windows machine:

shellCopy code

```
netstat -ano
```

By regularly collecting and analyzing statistics like network traffic volume, port usage, and packet counts, organizations can establish baseline values and detect anomalies when network metrics deviate significantly from these baselines.

Behavioral analysis is another technique used to identify anomalies in network traffic.

This approach focuses on understanding the typical behavior of network users, devices, and applications.

Behavioral analysis tools and solutions use machine learning algorithms to establish patterns of normal behavior and raise alerts when deviations occur.

For instance, user and entity behavior analytics (UEBA) solutions analyze user and entity activities to detect suspicious activities, such as unauthorized access or data exfiltration.

To deploy UEBA solutions, organizations typically need to install and configure specialized software or appliances and integrate them with existing security infrastructure.

Once implemented, these solutions continuously monitor user and entity activities and raise alerts when they detect unusual behavior.

Signature-based detection is a technique that relies on predefined signatures or patterns of known threats to identify anomalies in network traffic.

Intrusion detection systems (IDS) and intrusion prevention systems (IPS) use signature-based detection to recognize known attack patterns and alert or block traffic associated with those patterns.

For example, the open-source IDS Snort uses rule-based signatures to detect known threats in network traffic.

To deploy Snort, organizations can follow these steps:

Install Snort on a dedicated server or device.

Create custom rule sets or download rule sets from trusted sources.

Configure Snort to monitor specific network interfaces or segments.

Analyze alerts generated by Snort to identify anomalies and potential threats.

Heuristic analysis is a technique that goes beyond predefined signatures and uses heuristics or rules to identify suspicious or potentially malicious behavior.

This approach allows organizations to detect new or previously unknown threats based on their behavior rather than relying solely on known patterns.

For example, heuristic analysis can identify anomalies such as excessive file access, unusual login patterns, or unexpected data transfers.

To deploy heuristic analysis, organizations often use advanced security information and event management (SIEM) systems that incorporate heuristic-based detection capabilities.

SIEM solutions collect and analyze log data from various sources, including network devices, servers, and endpoints, to identify anomalies and generate alerts.

To configure and deploy a SIEM system, organizations typically need to:

Select a suitable SIEM solution based on their requirements and budget.

Install and configure the SIEM software or appliance.

Integrate the SIEM system with their network infrastructure and security devices.

Define correlation rules and thresholds to identify anomalies.

Set up alerting mechanisms and response workflows to act upon detected anomalies.

Anomaly detection can also extend to the analysis of DNS traffic, which can reveal malicious activities like domain generation algorithms (DGA) used by certain malware.

Analyzing DNS logs and traffic patterns can help identify unusual domain requests, spikes in DNS traffic, or patterns consistent with known malicious activity.

To analyze DNS traffic, organizations can use tools like "dnstop" to monitor DNS statistics in real-time:

shellCopy code

```
dnstop -l 5 eth0
```

In addition to the technical aspects of anomaly detection, organizations should establish clear incident response processes and procedures for when anomalies are detected.

These processes should define how security teams respond to alerts generated by anomaly detection systems, including investigation, containment, eradication, and recovery steps.

Regular training and drills for incident response teams help ensure that they are well-prepared to handle anomalies effectively.

Furthermore, organizations can leverage threat intelligence feeds and information-sharing platforms to enhance their anomaly detection capabilities.

Threat intelligence provides valuable insights into emerging threats and known attack patterns, allowing organizations to fine-tune their anomaly detection systems to focus on specific threats relevant to their industry or region.

To integrate threat intelligence feeds into their anomaly detection process, organizations typically need to:

Identify trusted threat intelligence sources or providers.

Subscribe to relevant threat intelligence feeds.

Develop or configure rules and indicators based on threat intelligence data.

Regularly update and maintain threat intelligence feeds and indicators.

In summary, identifying anomalies in network traffic is a critical part of maintaining a strong cybersecurity posture.

By combining statistical analysis, behavioral analysis, signature-based detection, heuristic analysis, and DNS traffic analysis, organizations can effectively detect and respond to anomalies that may indicate security threats.

Additionally, clear incident response processes, training, and the integration of threat intelligence can further enhance an organization's ability to detect and mitigate security incidents.

Chapter 6: Behavioral Analytics for Threat Detection

User and Entity Behavior Analytics (UEBA) is a sophisticated cybersecurity approach that focuses on monitoring and analyzing the behavior of users, devices, and entities within an organization's network to detect and respond to security threats.

UEBA leverages machine learning algorithms and statistical analysis to establish baseline behavior patterns for individuals and entities and then identifies deviations from these baselines, which may indicate suspicious or malicious activities.

To implement UEBA effectively, organizations typically deploy specialized software solutions that integrate with their existing security infrastructure.

One commonly used UEBA tool is Splunk User Behavior Analytics (UBA), which provides a platform for monitoring and analyzing user and entity behavior.

To set up Splunk UBA, organizations can follow these steps:

Install and configure the Splunk UBA software on dedicated servers or virtual machines within their network.

Connect Splunk UBA to relevant data sources, including logs from network devices, servers, endpoints, and applications.

Define user and entity profiles, specifying the behavior patterns considered normal for different roles and entities within the organization.

Allow the system to learn and establish baselines by analyzing historical data and behavior patterns.

Configure alerting rules and thresholds to trigger notifications when deviations from normal behavior are detected.

Regularly review and investigate alerts to identify potential security threats and respond accordingly.

One of the primary advantages of UEBA is its ability to detect insider threats, which are often more challenging to identify using traditional security measures.

UEBA solutions can spot unusual or suspicious activities by employees or entities, such as unauthorized data access, data exfiltration, or privilege escalation, that may indicate malicious intent or compromised accounts.

Furthermore, UEBA can help organizations uncover security incidents that involve compromised user credentials, such as credential theft or brute-force attacks.

By monitoring user behavior and detecting anomalies, UEBA solutions can quickly identify unauthorized access attempts and take proactive measures to protect sensitive data.

UEBA also plays a crucial role in identity and access management by continuously evaluating user and entity behavior to ensure that access privileges remain appropriate and secure.

Organizations can use UEBA insights to fine-tune access controls, adjust permissions, and promptly revoke access when suspicious or high-risk behavior is detected.

In addition to monitoring user and entity behavior, UEBA solutions often provide a comprehensive view of security incidents by correlating data from various sources and identifying patterns or relationships between events.

This correlation allows organizations to gain a holistic understanding of potential threats, enabling them to respond more effectively.

While UEBA can be a valuable asset in enhancing an organization's security posture, it is not without its challenges.

One challenge is the need for a substantial amount of data for effective machine learning and baseline establishment.

Organizations may struggle to collect, store, and manage the extensive data required to create accurate behavior profiles.

To address this challenge, organizations should plan for sufficient data storage and implement data retention policies that align with their UEBA objectives.

Another challenge is the risk of false positives, where the system generates alerts for behavior that is not genuinely malicious.

False positives can lead to alert fatigue among security teams and divert resources away from genuine threats.

To mitigate this risk, organizations should fine-tune their UEBA systems, adjust alerting thresholds, and invest in contextual analysis to provide additional context to alerts.

Moreover, UEBA solutions often require ongoing tuning and refinement to adapt to evolving user and entity behavior patterns and emerging threats.

To address this, organizations should establish processes for regular assessment and optimization of their UEBA systems.

In summary, User and Entity Behavior Analytics (UEBA) is a powerful cybersecurity approach that leverages machine learning and statistical analysis to monitor and analyze the behavior of users, devices, and entities within an organization's network.

By establishing behavior baselines and identifying deviations from these baselines, UEBA solutions can help organizations detect and respond to security threats, including insider threats, compromised credentials, and unauthorized access attempts.

While UEBA offers significant benefits in terms of threat detection and response, organizations must also address challenges related to data collection, false positives, and ongoing system tuning to maximize its effectiveness.

Predictive analytics is a powerful tool in the realm of cybersecurity, enabling organizations to proactively identify and mitigate potential threats before they manifest into security incidents.

This approach involves using historical data, statistical algorithms, machine learning models, and data mining techniques to forecast future cybersecurity events and trends.

To implement predictive analytics in cybersecurity effectively, organizations need to collect and analyze large volumes of data from various sources, including logs, network traffic, user behavior, and threat intelligence feeds.

This data serves as the foundation for training predictive models that can identify patterns and anomalies indicative of emerging threats.

One common application of predictive analytics in cybersecurity is the prediction of malware outbreaks.

By analyzing historical malware infection data, organizations can develop models that identify patterns in malware propagation, helping them anticipate and prepare for potential outbreaks.

To deploy predictive analytics for malware outbreak prediction, organizations can follow these steps:

Gather historical malware infection data, including timestamps, affected systems, malware types, and infection vectors.

Preprocess and clean the data to remove noise and inconsistencies.

Feature engineering involves selecting relevant attributes or features from the data that are indicative of malware infections, such as the frequency of user downloads, email attachments, or system vulnerabilities.

Choose a suitable machine learning algorithm, such as logistic regression, decision trees, or neural networks, and train the model using the prepared data.

Validate the model's performance using separate datasets and fine-tune it to improve accuracy.

Deploy the predictive model in a real-time or near-real-time environment, where it continuously monitors incoming data for signs of potential malware outbreaks.

Implement alerting mechanisms to notify security teams when the predictive model identifies a high-risk situation.

Predictive analytics can also be employed to forecast other types of cyber threats, such as distributed denial-of-service (DDoS) attacks.

By analyzing historical DDoS attack data, organizations can develop models that predict when and where future attacks are likely to occur.

These models can consider factors like IP traffic patterns, geographic origins of attack traffic, and vulnerabilities in network infrastructure.

To implement predictive analytics for DDoS attack prediction, organizations can:

Collect historical DDoS attack data, including attack vectors, durations, targets, and attack sources.

Prepare the data for analysis by cleaning and structuring it appropriately.

Use machine learning algorithms, such as clustering or time series analysis, to identify patterns and trends in the historical data.

Train predictive models to recognize characteristics of impending DDoS attacks, such as sudden increases in traffic from specific geographic regions.

Validate and fine-tune the models to reduce false positives and improve accuracy.

Integrate the predictive analytics system into the network infrastructure to monitor incoming traffic and detect potential DDoS attack patterns.

Implement automated mitigation measures, such as traffic filtering or rate limiting, when the predictive model signals a likely DDoS attack.

Predictive analytics can also enhance insider threat detection by analyzing user behavior and identifying anomalies indicative of malicious intent or compromised accounts.

For instance, if an organization's predictive model detects a sudden increase in an employee's access to sensitive data or an unusual pattern of file downloads, it may trigger an alert for further investigation.

To implement predictive analytics for insider threat detection, organizations can:

Collect user activity logs, access timestamps, file access history, and other relevant user behavior data.

Prepare the data by cleaning and normalizing it to facilitate analysis.

Develop predictive models that can identify deviations from normal user behavior, such as unauthorized data access or unusual login patterns.

Train the models on historical user behavior data and validate their performance using test datasets.

Integrate the predictive analytics system into the organization's security infrastructure to continuously monitor user activities and generate alerts when anomalies are detected.

Implement response workflows for incident investigation and mitigation when insider threats are identified.

Predictive analytics is not limited to threat prediction alone but can also be applied to vulnerability management.

Organizations can use predictive models to forecast which vulnerabilities are most likely to be exploited by attackers based on historical vulnerability data, severity scores, and exploitability factors.

To implement predictive analytics for vulnerability management, organizations can:

Collect historical vulnerability data, including details about vulnerabilities, Common Vulnerability Scoring System (CVSS) scores, and exploit availability.

Prepare the data by cleaning and structuring it for analysis.

Use machine learning algorithms or statistical models to identify patterns that indicate which vulnerabilities are more likely to be targeted.

Train the predictive models on historical data, validate their performance, and fine-tune them to improve accuracy.

Integrate the predictive analytics system with vulnerability assessment tools and data sources to continuously assess and prioritize vulnerabilities based on the predictive model's insights.

Implement a remediation strategy that focuses on addressing the most likely-to-be-exploited vulnerabilities first.

In summary, predictive analytics is a valuable approach in cybersecurity that empowers organizations to anticipate and proactively respond to potential threats and vulnerabilities.

By harnessing historical data, machine learning algorithms, and statistical analysis, organizations can develop predictive models that enhance their ability to forecast and mitigate cybersecurity risks effectively.

Whether applied to malware outbreak prediction, DDoS attack forecasting, insider threat detection, or vulnerability management, predictive analytics plays a vital role in modern cybersecurity strategies.

Chapter 7: Intrusion Detection Systems (IDS) and Intrusion Prevention Systems (IPS)

Intrusion Detection Systems (IDS) and Intrusion Prevention Systems (IPS) are essential components of modern cybersecurity strategies, helping organizations detect and respond to potential threats and attacks in real-time.

There are various types of IDS and IPS, each with its unique characteristics and deployment considerations.

Network-Based IDS (NIDS) is a type of IDS that monitors network traffic and analyzes data packets to identify suspicious or malicious activities.

NIDS are typically placed at strategic points within a network, such as network gateways or segments, and they passively inspect incoming and outgoing traffic.

To deploy a NIDS, organizations often use specialized hardware appliances or software solutions.

One well-known open-source NIDS is Snort, which uses signature-based detection to identify known attack patterns in network traffic.

To set up Snort as a NIDS, organizations can follow these steps:

Install Snort on a dedicated server or appliance within the network.

Configure Snort to monitor specific network interfaces or segments.

Create custom or download pre-defined rulesets to detect specific threats or attack patterns.

Configure alerting mechanisms to notify security teams when suspicious activity is detected.

Host-Based IDS (HIDS) is designed to monitor the activity and security of individual host systems, such as servers, workstations, and endpoints.

HIDS solutions operate on the host itself, monitoring system logs, file integrity, registry changes, and other host-specific events.

To deploy a HIDS, organizations typically install specialized agents or software on each host they wish to protect.

One popular HIDS solution is OSSEC, an open-source host-based intrusion detection system.

To set up OSSEC as a HIDS, organizations can perform the following steps:

Install the OSSEC agent on each host system.

Configure the agent to monitor the host's logs, files, and system events.

Define custom rules or use pre-configured rules to identify suspicious activities.

Configure alerting mechanisms to notify security teams or a central monitoring server when incidents occur.

Hybrid IDS (HIDS/NIDS) combines elements of both Network-Based IDS (NIDS) and Host-Based IDS (HIDS) to provide comprehensive intrusion detection capabilities.

This type of IDS integrates network monitoring with host-level monitoring, allowing for a holistic view of security events across the network.

Hybrid IDS solutions are well-suited for organizations that require both network-wide threat detection and host-level security monitoring.

To deploy a Hybrid IDS, organizations must implement both NIDS and HIDS components, ensuring they are configured to work together seamlessly.

For example, a NIDS may detect suspicious network traffic and correlate it with HIDS data from affected host systems to provide a more complete picture of a potential security incident.

Signature-Based Detection is a widely used technique in IDS and IPS solutions.

It involves matching patterns or signatures of known threats or attack behaviors against incoming or outgoing network traffic.

Signature-based detection relies on extensive databases of threat signatures, and it is effective at identifying well-known attack patterns.

However, it may struggle with detecting zero-day attacks or attacks that have not been previously documented.

To illustrate the concept of signature-based detection, consider an IDS or IPS that uses a signature to identify a specific type of malware by examining patterns within network packets.

When the system encounters network traffic that matches the malware signature, it generates an alert or takes preventive action, such as blocking the malicious traffic.

Anomaly-Based Detection is a technique used to identify deviations from established baselines or normal behavior patterns.

Rather than relying on known threat signatures, anomaly-based detection systems analyze network or host behavior to detect unusual activities that may indicate a security incident.

This approach is particularly effective at detecting zero-day attacks and insider threats that do not exhibit known attack patterns.

To illustrate anomaly-based detection, consider a NIDS that monitors network traffic and establishes baselines for various network metrics, such as packet rates, connection durations, or data transfer volumes.

When the system observes network behavior that significantly deviates from these baselines, it generates an alert, indicating a potential security anomaly.

Behavioral Analysis is an advanced form of anomaly-based detection that focuses on understanding the behavior of users, devices, and entities within a network.

Behavioral analysis systems establish baselines for individual or entity behavior patterns and identify deviations that may indicate suspicious or malicious activities.

This approach is particularly effective for insider threat detection and identifying unusual user behavior.

To implement behavioral analysis, organizations collect and analyze data related to user activities, access patterns, and data transfers.

Machine learning algorithms and statistical models are then used to establish and update behavior baselines for users and entities.

When deviations from these baselines are detected, the system generates alerts or triggers automated responses.

To provide an example of behavioral analysis, consider a HIDS that monitors user activities on a server.

The HIDS establishes a baseline for normal user behavior, including login times, file access patterns, and command executions.

If a user's behavior suddenly changes, such as accessing sensitive files or executing unusual commands, the HIDS may generate an alert, as this deviation could indicate unauthorized or malicious activity.

Protocol-Based Detection focuses on identifying malicious activities based on deviations from expected network protocols and behaviors.

Protocol-based detection systems analyze network traffic to ensure that it adheres to the standard protocols and behaviors defined for various services and applications.

When deviations or protocol violations are detected, the system raises alerts or takes preventive actions.

For example, a NIDS using protocol-based detection may monitor the behavior of the Simple Mail Transfer Protocol (SMTP) to detect anomalies in email traffic.

If the system observes SMTP traffic that does not conform to the expected protocol specifications, such as an unusual sequence of SMTP commands or excessive data transfer rates, it may generate an alert, indicating a potential email-based attack.

Statistical Analysis involves the use of statistical methods and algorithms to identify anomalies or patterns in network or host behavior.

Statistical analysis techniques can detect deviations from expected statistical distributions, helping to identify potential security incidents.

To implement statistical analysis, organizations collect relevant data, such as network traffic statistics, system performance metrics, or user access patterns.

They then apply statistical models and algorithms to analyze the data and identify anomalies.

If the statistical analysis detects anomalies that exceed predefined thresholds, the system generates alerts for further investigation.

To illustrate statistical analysis, consider a NIDS that monitors network traffic statistics, such as packet size distributions or connection rates.

The NIDS uses statistical models to establish expected distributions for these metrics.

When it observes network traffic that significantly deviates from these expected distributions, such as an unusually high number of large packets or a rapid increase in connection rates, it generates alerts, suggesting potential anomalies or attacks.

Intrusion Detection Systems (IDS) and Intrusion Prevention Systems (IPS) play a crucial role in safeguarding network and host systems against cybersecurity threats.

These systems can be categorized into Network-Based IDS (NIDS), Host-Based IDS (HIDS), Hybrid IDS (HIDS/NIDS), each with its unique monitoring capabilities and deployment considerations.

Signature-Based Detection relies on matching patterns or signatures of known threats against network traffic, while Anomaly-Based Detection identifies deviations from established baselines or normal behavior.

Behavioral Analysis takes anomaly detection a step further by focusing on understanding user and entity behavior within a network.

Protocol-Based Detection monitors network traffic to ensure adherence to standard protocols, while Statistical Analysis applies statistical methods to identify anomalies or patterns in network or host behavior.

Ultimately, the choice of IDS and IPS types and techniques depends on an organization's specific security requirements and the nature of the threats it aims to detect and prevent.

Signature-based detection and behavioral-based detection are two fundamental approaches in the field of cybersecurity, each offering unique advantages and limitations in identifying and mitigating security threats.

Signature-based detection relies on predefined patterns or signatures of known threats, making it effective at identifying and blocking well-documented attacks and malware.

To illustrate this concept, consider an antivirus software that uses signature-based detection.

When a file or program is scanned, the antivirus compares its digital signature, hash, or code patterns against a database of known malicious signatures.

If a match is found, the antivirus flags the file as malicious and takes appropriate action, such as quarantining or deleting it.

Signature-based detection is widely used and highly efficient in detecting known threats, providing organizations with a reliable defense against well-established malware and attack techniques.

However, this approach has limitations, as it struggles to identify new or previously unseen threats, often referred to as "zero-day" vulnerabilities or attacks.

Because signature-based detection relies on matching against known signatures, it cannot detect attacks that have not been documented and added to its signature database.

To mitigate this limitation, cybersecurity professionals and organizations must regularly update their signature databases to stay current with emerging threats.

Behavioral-based detection, on the other hand, takes a different approach by analyzing the behavior of files, applications, users, and systems to identify anomalies and potential threats.

This technique is particularly effective at detecting zero-day attacks and sophisticated threats that may not exhibit known attack patterns.

To implement behavioral-based detection, consider an Intrusion Detection System (IDS) that monitors network traffic.

Instead of relying solely on signature matching, the IDS establishes baselines for normal network behavior, such as traffic patterns, packet rates, and access behavior.

The IDS then continuously monitors network traffic and alerts security teams when deviations from these baselines are detected.

For example, if an employee's workstation suddenly starts sending a large volume of data to an external IP address or exhibits unusual access patterns, the IDS may generate an alert.

Behavioral-based detection relies on anomaly detection algorithms, machine learning, and statistical analysis to identify suspicious activities.

This approach excels at detecting unknown or polymorphic malware that may change its code to evade signature-based detection.

Moreover, behavioral-based detection is highly adaptable and can learn and adjust to evolving threats over time.

While signature-based detection may generate false positives in certain cases, behavioral-based detection can help minimize false positives by focusing on unusual activities that deviate from established behavior baselines.

To deploy behavioral-based detection effectively, organizations should:

Collect and aggregate data from various sources, including network traffic, endpoint logs, user behavior, and system events.

Establish baseline behavior patterns for different entities within the organization, such as users, devices, and applications.

Implement machine learning models or statistical analysis techniques to continuously evaluate incoming data for deviations from these baselines.

Configure alerting mechanisms to notify security teams when anomalies are detected.

Regularly update and fine-tune behavioral-based detection systems to adapt to changing environments and evolving threats.

One common use case for behavioral-based detection is User and Entity Behavior Analytics (UEBA), which focuses on monitoring user and entity activities to detect insider threats, compromised accounts, and unusual behavior.

UEBA solutions establish baselines for normal behavior patterns for users, devices, and entities within an organization.

When deviations from these baselines are identified, the system generates alerts or takes automated actions to mitigate potential threats.

For instance, if a user suddenly accesses sensitive files they have never accessed before or exhibits unusual login patterns, the UEBA system may flag these activities as suspicious and alert the security team.

In summary, signature-based detection and behavioral-based detection are two essential approaches in cybersecurity, each with its strengths and weaknesses.

Signature-based detection excels at identifying known threats and is highly efficient in providing protection against well-documented attacks and malware.

However, it may struggle to detect new or previously unseen threats.

Behavioral-based detection, on the other hand, focuses on analyzing behavior patterns and identifying anomalies, making it effective at detecting zero-day attacks and sophisticated threats.

Organizations often deploy a combination of both techniques to provide comprehensive security coverage, leveraging the strengths of each approach to enhance their cybersecurity posture.

Chapter 8: Advanced Malware Analysis and Reverse Engineering

Dynamic malware analysis is a crucial process in cybersecurity that involves running and observing malicious software, such as malware and viruses, in a controlled environment to understand its behavior and functionality.

One of the primary objectives of dynamic malware analysis is to dissect and analyze the malware's activities, allowing cybersecurity professionals to develop effective countermeasures and protect against future threats.

Dynamic analysis is particularly valuable for dealing with unknown or zero-day malware, which lacks known signatures or patterns that can be detected by traditional antivirus software.

To perform dynamic malware analysis, security researchers and analysts often use specialized environments called "sandboxes" that isolate the malware and its activities from the host system. These sandboxes emulate a controlled computing environment where the malware can execute and reveal its behavior without harming the actual systems.

One popular open-source sandbox for dynamic malware analysis is Cuckoo Sandbox, which can be installed and used on a Linux-based system.

To set up Cuckoo Sandbox, follow these steps:

Install a clean and isolated virtual machine or physical host system for running the sandbox.

Install the required dependencies, such as Python, MongoDB, and various analysis tools, on the host system.

Download and configure Cuckoo Sandbox on the host system.

Define the analysis environment, including the operating system and software configurations you want to use for executing malware samples.

Configure the analysis system to route network traffic through a controlled environment for monitoring.

Submit malware samples to the Cuckoo Sandbox for analysis.

Once the malware is executed within the sandbox, dynamic analysis tools monitor its behavior, such as file system changes, registry modifications, network communications, and system process interactions.

One of the critical aspects of dynamic malware analysis is the ability to capture and analyze the malware's network traffic.

To capture network traffic during dynamic analysis, you can use a packet capture tool like Wireshark, which allows you to monitor the network interactions of the malware.

For example, in a Linux-based environment, you can use the "tcpdump" command to capture network packets generated by the malware. Here's a CLI command to start a packet capture:

cssCopy code

```
sudo tcpdump -i eth0 -w malware_traffic.pcap
```

This command captures network traffic on the "eth0" network interface and saves it to a file named "malware_traffic.pcap."

Analyzing the captured network traffic can provide valuable insights into the malware's communication with command and control servers, data exfiltration, and potential vulnerabilities it may exploit.

Another critical aspect of dynamic malware analysis is monitoring the malware's system interactions, including file system modifications and registry changes.

Tools like Process Monitor for Windows or the "strace" command for Linux can be used to track these interactions.

For instance, the "strace" command in Linux allows you to trace system calls made by a running process, which can help identify the files the malware creates, modifies, or deletes. Here's an example CLI command:

bashCopy code

```
strace -f -e trace=file -o malware_file_operations.txt ./malware_sample
```

This command traces file-related system calls of the "malware_sample" executable and saves the output to a text file named "malware_file_operations.txt."

Analyzing the file system and registry changes performed by the malware is essential for understanding its impact on the compromised system and for developing effective remediation strategies.

Additionally, dynamic analysis often involves monitoring the malware's behavior related to process creation and memory manipulation.

Tools like Process Explorer for Windows or the "gdb" debugger for Linux can be useful for tracking these aspects of malware behavior.

For example, you can use the "gdb" debugger to attach to a running malware process and inspect its memory and execution flow. Here's an example CLI command:

cssCopy code

```
gdb -p <malware_process_id>
```

Replace "<malware_process_id>" with the actual process ID of the running malware.

By inspecting the malware's memory and analyzing its execution flow, analysts can gain insights into its evasion techniques, payload decryption routines, and other critical behaviors.

In dynamic malware analysis, behavioral analysis is a crucial component that involves observing the malware's actions and interactions with the host system and its environment.

Analysts look for signs of malicious intent, such as attempts to steal sensitive data, establish unauthorized network connections, escalate privileges, or evade detection.

Behavioral analysis often requires a deep understanding of operating system internals and malware analysis techniques to interpret the observed behavior accurately.

To facilitate behavioral analysis, analysts may use tools like the Sysinternals Suite for Windows or similar utilities for other operating systems.

For instance, Process Explorer, part of the Sysinternals Suite, provides detailed information about running processes, including their associated threads, network activity, and loaded modules.

By closely monitoring process behavior and interactions, analysts can identify suspicious or malicious activities that may not be immediately apparent.

Another aspect of behavioral analysis is examining the malware's persistence mechanisms, which allow it to maintain a presence on the compromised system even after a reboot.

Common persistence techniques include adding malicious entries to the Windows Registry, creating startup scripts, or injecting malicious code into legitimate processes.

To investigate persistence mechanisms during dynamic malware analysis, analysts may use tools like Autoruns for Windows or similar utilities.

Autoruns provides a comprehensive view of all startup programs, services, and registry entries, making it easier to identify and analyze suspicious persistence mechanisms.

In summary, dynamic malware analysis is a critical process in cybersecurity that involves executing and observing malicious software in a controlled environment to understand its behavior and functionality.

This analysis is particularly valuable for dealing with unknown or zero-day malware that lacks known signatures.

To perform dynamic malware analysis, analysts often use sandboxes that isolate the malware, monitoring its behavior, network interactions, file system modifications, and more.

Tools like Wireshark, Process Monitor, and the Sysinternals Suite are essential for capturing and analyzing network traffic, tracking system interactions, and conducting behavioral analysis.

By thoroughly analyzing the behavior of malware, cybersecurity professionals can gain insights into its capabilities, intent, and potential impact, allowing them to develop effective countermeasures and protect against future threats.

Reverse engineering malicious code is a complex and essential process in cybersecurity, allowing analysts to understand the inner workings of malware and develop effective countermeasures.
This technique involves taking apart malicious software to dissect its functionality, reveal its intent, and identify vulnerabilities it may exploit.
One of the primary goals of reverse engineering malicious code is to extract valuable information about the malware's behavior, such as its propagation methods, communication with command and control servers, and data exfiltration mechanisms.
To begin reverse engineering, analysts often start with a sample of the malicious code, which can be obtained from infected systems or malware repositories.
Once a sample is acquired, it can be loaded into a specialized analysis environment or sandbox, ensuring that it operates in an isolated and controlled environment that protects the analyst's system.
In a Linux-based environment, analysts can use the "strings" command to extract readable strings from the binary file, which can provide clues about the malware's functionality.
For example, the following CLI command extracts strings from a binary file named "malware_sample":
Copy code

```
strings malware_sample
```

The "strings" command can reveal text strings embedded in the malware, such as URLs, filenames, or cryptographic keys, which can be critical for understanding its behavior and communication patterns.

Another essential technique in reverse engineering is static analysis, which involves examining the malware's code and structure without executing it.

Static analysis techniques include disassembling the binary code to produce assembly language representation and analyzing its control flow and data structures.

To disassemble a binary file, analysts can use tools like IDA Pro or objdump for Linux.

For instance, to disassemble a binary file named "malware_sample" using objdump, you can use the following CLI command:

arduinoCopy code

```
objdump -d malware_sample > disassembled_code.asm
```

This command generates an assembly language listing in the "disassembled_code.asm" file, allowing analysts to study the code's logic and operations.

Static analysis also involves examining the malware's headers, import/export tables, and other structural elements to identify potential indicators of compromise (IOCs) and behavioral patterns.

To gain insights into the malware's behavior, analysts may focus on specific functions or code segments that are responsible for critical actions, such as network communication or file manipulation.

By reverse engineering these segments, analysts can uncover how the malware operates and identify opportunities for mitigation.

Dynamic analysis is another crucial aspect of reverse engineering malicious code, involving the execution of the malware within a controlled environment to observe its behavior.

Dynamic analysis allows analysts to monitor the malware's actions in real-time, such as file system changes, registry modifications, and network communications.

To set up a dynamic analysis environment, analysts often use sandboxes or virtual machines (VMs) that isolate the malware from the host system.

Once the malware is executed within this controlled environment, analysts can use monitoring tools to capture its behavior.

For example, in a Linux-based environment, analysts can use the "strace" command to trace system calls made by the malware process:

bashCopy code

```
strace -f -o malware_behavior.txt ./malware_sample
```

This command traces system calls and saves the output to a text file named "malware_behavior.txt."

Dynamic analysis can reveal how the malware interacts with the compromised system and whether it exhibits evasion techniques to avoid detection.

It also provides insights into the malware's network traffic, including communication with command and control servers and data exfiltration.

Behavioral analysis is a critical component of dynamic analysis, focusing on observing the malware's actions, such as attempts to steal sensitive data, establish unauthorized network connections, escalate privileges, or evade detection.

Behavioral analysis often requires a deep understanding of operating system internals and malware analysis techniques to interpret the observed behavior accurately.

To facilitate behavioral analysis, analysts may use tools like Process Explorer for Windows or similar utilities for other operating systems.

For instance, Process Explorer provides detailed information about running processes, their associated threads, network activity, and loaded modules.

By closely monitoring process behavior and interactions, analysts can identify suspicious or malicious activities that may not be immediately apparent.

Another aspect of behavioral analysis is examining the malware's persistence mechanisms, which allow it to maintain a presence on the compromised system even after a reboot.

Persistence techniques include adding malicious entries to the Windows Registry, creating startup scripts, or injecting malicious code into legitimate processes.

To investigate persistence mechanisms, analysts may use tools like Autoruns for Windows or similar utilities.

Autoruns provides a comprehensive view of all startup programs, services, and registry entries, making it easier to identify and analyze suspicious persistence mechanisms.

In summary, reverse engineering malicious code is a crucial process in cybersecurity that involves dissecting and analyzing malware to understand its functionality, behavior, and vulnerabilities.

Static analysis techniques, such as disassembling code and examining structural elements, help analysts gain insights into the malware's logic and operations.

Dynamic analysis, conducted within controlled environments, allows analysts to observe the malware's behavior, including system interactions and network communications.

Behavioral analysis focuses on monitoring the malware's actions and identifying signs of malicious intent or evasion techniques.

By combining these techniques, cybersecurity professionals can unravel the inner workings of malicious code, develop effective countermeasures, and protect against future threats.

Chapter 9: Incident Response and Cybersecurity Incident Handling

Incident response frameworks are essential in the field of cybersecurity, providing organizations with structured approaches to managing and mitigating security incidents.

These frameworks serve as a blueprint for how organizations should respond to incidents, ensuring that they can effectively detect, analyze, contain, and recover from security breaches.

One of the widely recognized incident response frameworks is the NIST (National Institute of Standards and Technology) Cybersecurity Framework.

The NIST Cybersecurity Framework provides a set of guidelines and best practices for organizations to manage and improve their cybersecurity posture.

This framework is based on five core functions: Identify, Protect, Detect, Respond, and Recover.

The "Identify" function focuses on understanding an organization's cybersecurity risks and vulnerabilities.

To implement this function, organizations can conduct asset inventory, risk assessments, and threat intelligence gathering.

One way to conduct a risk assessment is by using the Nmap (Network Mapper) tool, which can help identify open ports and services on networked devices.

For example, the following CLI command scans a target network and provides information about open ports:

cssCopy code

```
nmap -p- -T4 -oN scan_results.txt 192.168.1.0/24
```

In this command, "nmap" is the tool, "-p-" specifies scanning all 65,535 ports, "-T4" sets the scan speed to a higher level, "-oN" specifies the output format, and "192.168.1.0/24" represents the target IP range.

The "Protect" function focuses on implementing safeguards to limit or contain the impact of incidents.

This includes measures such as access controls, encryption, and security awareness training for employees.

The "Detect" function aims to identify incidents promptly through continuous monitoring and anomaly detection.

In this phase, organizations can use intrusion detection systems (IDS), security information and event management (SIEM) solutions, and log analysis tools to spot unusual activities.

For example, Snort is an open-source IDS that can be used to detect suspicious network traffic patterns.

To configure Snort, analysts can create custom rules to monitor specific network behaviors.

The "Respond" function involves taking immediate actions to mitigate the impact of an incident.

This includes isolating affected systems, applying patches or updates, and engaging law enforcement or incident response teams.

To contain a compromised system, analysts can use the "netsh" command in Windows to disable network interfaces temporarily:

vbnetCopy code

```
netsh interface set interface "Ethernet" admin=disable
```

In this command, "Ethernet" should be replaced with the actual network interface name.

The "Recover" function focuses on restoring normal operations after an incident.

This involves data recovery, system restoration, and a review of the incident response process to improve future responses.

Another well-known incident response framework is the SANS (SysAdmin, Audit, Network, Security) Institute's Incident Handler's Handbook.

The SANS framework provides practical guidance and steps for incident handling and response.

One of the core components of the SANS framework is the Incident Handling Process, which includes six stages: Preparation, Identification, Containment, Eradication, Recovery, and Lessons Learned.

The "Preparation" stage involves establishing an incident response team, defining procedures, and ensuring that necessary tools and resources are available.

The "Identification" stage focuses on recognizing and confirming the occurrence of an incident.

During this stage, organizations may deploy intrusion detection systems, log analysis tools, and endpoint security solutions to identify signs of a security breach.

The "Containment" stage aims to prevent the incident from spreading further and causing additional damage.

This can involve isolating affected systems, disabling compromised accounts, or blocking malicious network traffic.

The "Eradication" stage focuses on completely removing the root cause of the incident.

This may involve patching vulnerabilities, removing malware, and eliminating unauthorized access.

The "Recovery" stage is about restoring systems and services to normal operation.

This includes verifying the integrity of data, reinstalling clean operating systems, and monitoring for any signs of re-infection.

The "Lessons Learned" stage is essential for continuous improvement.

Organizations should conduct post-incident reviews to identify weaknesses in their incident response process and take corrective actions.

In addition to the NIST and SANS frameworks, there are other incident response frameworks tailored to specific industries and regulatory requirements.

For example, the Payment Card Industry Data Security Standard (PCI DSS) provides guidelines for organizations handling payment card data.

The Health Insurance Portability and Accountability Act (HIPAA) offers incident response guidance for healthcare organizations. Furthermore, international standards like ISO/IEC 27035 provide a comprehensive approach to incident management.

In summary, incident response frameworks are essential tools for organizations to effectively manage and mitigate security incidents.

These frameworks provide structured approaches and best practices for identifying, protecting, detecting, responding to, and recovering from incidents.

By following established incident response frameworks and utilizing appropriate tools and techniques, organizations can enhance their cybersecurity posture and minimize the impact of security breaches. Cybersecurity incident handling is a critical aspect of an organization's overall security strategy, encompassing a set of best practices and procedures designed to detect, respond to, and recover from security incidents.

Incidents can range from malware infections and data breaches to denial-of-service attacks and insider threats, and organizations must be well-prepared to effectively handle these events. One of the fundamental best practices in cybersecurity incident handling is establishing a well-defined incident response plan.

This plan should outline the roles and responsibilities of the incident response team, define the incident classification and severity levels, and provide a step-by-step process for handling different types of incidents.

In addition to defining the plan, organizations should regularly test and update it to ensure that it remains effective in addressing evolving threats.

Regular training and awareness programs are another crucial aspect of incident handling best practices.

All employees, not just the incident response team, should be educated about security policies, the importance of reporting suspicious activities, and how to respond in the event of a security incident.

Employees should also be aware of the various communication channels available for reporting incidents, such as incident reporting forms, hotlines, or direct contact with the incident response team.

Effective communication is a cornerstone of incident handling, and organizations should have clear and established communication protocols.

This includes establishing communication channels for internal teams, such as IT, legal, and management, as well as external parties like law enforcement, regulatory bodies, and affected customers.

Clear communication is essential for coordinating incident response efforts, sharing critical information, and meeting legal and regulatory reporting requirements.

One of the initial steps in incident handling is detection, and organizations should employ robust monitoring and detection tools and techniques to identify security incidents as early as possible.

Intrusion detection systems (IDS), intrusion prevention systems (IPS), and security information and event management (SIEM) systems play a vital role in monitoring network traffic, analyzing logs, and alerting security teams to potential threats.

Regularly reviewing and analyzing logs and alerts is essential for identifying unusual or suspicious activities that may indicate an incident.

Security teams should establish automated alerts based on predefined criteria to expedite the detection of security incidents.

Incident response teams should also conduct tabletop exercises and simulated incident scenarios to test the organization's incident response capabilities.

These exercises help train the team and familiarize them with the incident response plan, ensuring that they are well-prepared to handle real incidents.

Incident response teams should have access to a well-equipped incident response toolkit that includes a variety of tools and resources to aid in the investigation, containment, and recovery phases of incident handling.

These tools may include forensic analysis tools, network monitoring tools, malware analysis platforms, and backup and recovery solutions.

Forensic analysis tools, such as EnCase or Autopsy, enable the examination of compromised systems to determine the scope of an incident, identify the attack vector, and gather evidence for potential legal or law enforcement action.

Network monitoring tools like Wireshark help incident responders analyze network traffic patterns and identify unusual or malicious activities.

Malware analysis platforms, such as Cuckoo Sandbox or VirusTotal, assist in analyzing and dissecting malware samples to understand their functionality and behavior.

Backup and recovery solutions are essential for quickly restoring affected systems to normal operation after an incident.

It is crucial to have regular backups of critical data and systems to ensure business continuity.

Incident response teams should follow a structured incident handling process that typically consists of the following phases: preparation, identification, containment, eradication, recovery, and lessons learned.

The "preparation" phase involves establishing the incident response plan, training the response team, and acquiring the necessary tools and resources.

The "identification" phase focuses on detecting and confirming the occurrence of an incident, often through the use of intrusion detection systems, log analysis, and employee reporting. Once an incident is identified, the "containment" phase aims to limit the incident's impact by isolating affected systems or networks, disabling compromised accounts, and blocking malicious activities. The "eradication" phase involves completely removing the root cause of the incident, such as eliminating malware, patching vulnerabilities, and closing security gaps. After eradicating the threat, organizations can move into the "recovery" phase, which focuses on restoring systems, data, and services to normal operation.

This phase may include data restoration from backups, system patching, and thorough testing to ensure that the organization can resume business as usual.

Lastly, the "lessons learned" phase involves a post-incident review to assess the organization's response, identify areas for improvement, and update the incident response plan accordingly.

This phase is crucial for continuous improvement and strengthening the organization's cybersecurity posture.

In summary, cybersecurity incident handling best practices encompass a range of activities and strategies to effectively detect, respond to, and recover from security incidents.

Establishing a well-defined incident response plan, providing regular training and awareness, implementing robust monitoring and detection tools, and conducting tabletop exercises are all essential components of effective incident handling.

Additionally, incident response teams should have access to a comprehensive toolkit, follow a structured incident handling process, and prioritize communication and coordination both internally and externally.

By adhering to these best practices, organizations can minimize the impact of security incidents, protect their assets, and maintain the trust of their stakeholders.

Chapter 10: Threat Hunting and Advanced Detection Strategies

Proactive threat hunting is a cybersecurity approach that goes beyond traditional threat detection methods, aiming to actively search for and identify hidden threats within an organization's network and systems.

This technique is vital because it assumes that determined attackers are already within the network, attempting to evade detection.

Proactive threat hunting is a proactive approach to security, focused on finding threats before they can cause significant damage or data breaches.

One of the primary techniques in proactive threat hunting is the use of threat intelligence feeds and indicators of compromise (IOCs).

Threat intelligence feeds provide valuable information about known threats, including malware signatures, malicious IP addresses, and attack patterns.

These feeds can be integrated into security systems to automatically detect and block known threats.

Analysts can also use threat intelligence to proactively search for indicators of compromise within their network by querying logs and monitoring for known malicious activity.

To do this, they can use security information and event management (SIEM) systems or custom scripts to search for specific IOCs, such as IP addresses, domain names, or file hashes.

For example, analysts can use a SIEM system to search for any network traffic going to or from known malicious IP addresses: bashCopy code

```
source = "firewall_logs" dest_ip= "123.456.789.0/24"
```

This query would identify any network traffic to or from the specified IP address range, allowing analysts to investigate further.

Another proactive threat hunting technique involves anomaly detection.

This technique leverages machine learning algorithms and statistical analysis to identify unusual patterns or deviations from baseline behavior.

By monitoring network and system activity, analysts can identify anomalies that may indicate a security threat.

Anomalies could include unusual login patterns, excessive data transfer, or unexpected changes in system configurations.

For example, analysts can use machine learning models to analyze user login behavior.

If a user suddenly starts logging in from a different location or at unusual times, it may be indicative of a compromised account.

Advanced tools like Elastic Stack, Splunk, or custom scripts can be used to create anomaly detection rules and generate alerts when unusual behavior is detected.

Proactive threat hunters should also focus on lateral movement detection.

Lateral movement refers to an attacker's progression through a network after gaining initial access.

Attackers often move laterally to access more valuable assets or to maintain a foothold within the network.

To detect lateral movement, analysts can use techniques like network flow analysis and endpoint monitoring.

Network flow analysis involves examining the flow of data between different devices on the network.

By monitoring network traffic and looking for unusual patterns of communication between devices, analysts can identify potential lateral movement.

Endpoint monitoring involves tracking the activities and behaviors of individual devices or endpoints within the network.

Advanced endpoint detection and response (EDR) solutions provide real-time visibility into endpoint activities, allowing analysts to detect suspicious behaviors, such as privilege escalation or unauthorized access attempts.

To proactively hunt for lateral movement, analysts can use EDR solutions to monitor endpoint activities and look for signs of unauthorized access or suspicious activities.

For example, if an EDR solution detects a user trying to access multiple endpoints rapidly, it may indicate an attempt at lateral movement.

Another critical proactive threat hunting technique is threat hunting hunts.

These hunts involve targeted, manual searches for signs of compromise or unusual activity within the network.

Analysts use their knowledge of attacker tactics, techniques, and procedures (TTPs) to guide these hunts.

Hunters can create custom queries or scripts to search for specific indicators of compromise, behaviors, or attack patterns.

For example, if there is evidence of a phishing attack, analysts may proactively hunt for emails with specific characteristics, such as suspicious attachments or links.

They can use email logs and content inspection tools to search for these indicators.

To do this, they can run custom scripts or use built-in search capabilities in email security solutions to filter and search through email logs for specific criteria.

These proactive threat hunting hunts can be scheduled regularly to ensure continuous monitoring and detection of evolving threats.

In addition to these techniques, proactive threat hunting also involves continuous learning and adapting to new threats and attack techniques.

Analysts should stay updated on the latest threat intelligence and security research to understand emerging threats and vulnerabilities.

They should also collaborate with other security professionals and share knowledge and insights to improve their collective ability to proactively detect and respond to threats.

In summary, proactive threat hunting is a vital cybersecurity technique that goes beyond traditional threat detection methods.

It involves using threat intelligence feeds, anomaly detection, lateral movement detection, and targeted threat hunting hunts to actively search for hidden threats within an organization's network and systems.

By proactively hunting for threats, organizations can identify and respond to security incidents before they escalate, reducing the potential impact of cyberattacks.

Leveraging machine learning for detection is a powerful approach in the field of cybersecurity that offers the ability to detect and respond to threats more efficiently and accurately.

Machine learning involves the use of algorithms and statistical models to enable computer systems to learn from and make predictions or decisions based on data.

In the context of cybersecurity, machine learning can be applied to various aspects of threat detection and mitigation.

One of the key areas where machine learning is highly effective is in the detection of malware and other malicious software.

Traditional antivirus solutions rely on signature-based detection, which involves identifying known malware based on predefined signatures.

However, this approach has limitations as it cannot detect new or previously unknown malware variants.

Machine learning techniques, on the other hand, can analyze the behavior of files and processes to identify suspicious or malicious activities.

For example, machine learning models can be trained to analyze the behavior of executable files and identify patterns associated with malware.

To deploy such a technique, security teams can use machine learning frameworks like TensorFlow or scikit-learn to build and train their models.

They can feed the models with labeled datasets containing both malicious and benign files to teach the models to distinguish between the two.

Once the models are trained, they can be integrated into the organization's security infrastructure to continuously analyze files and flag any that exhibit behavior consistent with malware.

Another area where machine learning shines in cybersecurity is in the detection of anomalies within network traffic.

Traditional rule-based approaches for intrusion detection rely on predefined rules to identify known attack patterns.

However, these rules can be ineffective against new and sophisticated attacks.

Machine learning models can be trained to analyze network traffic and identify deviations from normal patterns, which could indicate an intrusion or attack.

To implement this technique, security teams can use network monitoring tools that support machine learning-based anomaly detection.

For example, they can use tools like Zeek (formerly known as Bro) to capture network traffic and then use machine learning models to analyze the data and identify anomalies.

These anomalies might include unusual spikes in data transfer, unexpected communication between devices, or patterns of behavior that deviate from the norm.

Machine learning is also valuable in user and entity behavior analytics (UEBA), where it can help identify suspicious user activities and potential insider threats.

By analyzing user behavior over time, machine learning models can establish baselines for normal behavior and raise alerts when deviations from these baselines occur.

Security teams can deploy UEBA solutions that leverage machine learning to monitor user activities across the organization's IT infrastructure.

For example, they can use a UEBA platform that integrates with Active Directory logs to monitor user logins, access patterns, and file usage.

Machine learning models within the UEBA platform can then identify unusual or risky behavior, such as unauthorized access attempts or data exfiltration.

Moreover, machine learning can enhance email security by improving the detection of phishing attacks and email-based threats.

Phishing attacks often involve convincing emails that trick users into clicking on malicious links or downloading malware.

Machine learning models can analyze the content and context of emails to identify suspicious characteristics.

Email security solutions can use machine learning to evaluate email content, sender reputation, and user behavior to determine the likelihood of an email being malicious.

Security teams can also employ machine learning to prioritize and automate incident response.

When a security incident occurs, such as a malware infection or a network intrusion, it's essential to respond quickly and effectively.

Machine learning can assist in automatically triaging and prioritizing incidents based on their severity and impact.

This allows security teams to focus their efforts on addressing the most critical threats first.

Security orchestration and automation platforms (SOAR) can be used to integrate machine learning models with incident response workflows.

These platforms can analyze incident data, assess the potential impact, and determine the appropriate response actions.

For example, a machine learning model integrated into a SOAR platform can help identify a ransomware attack by analyzing network traffic patterns and file behavior.

Upon detecting the ransomware, the SOAR platform can automatically isolate affected systems and trigger backup and recovery processes.

In addition to detection, machine learning also plays a role in fraud prevention and financial cybersecurity.

Financial institutions use machine learning models to detect unusual transactions or patterns of behavior that may indicate fraudulent activities.

Machine learning can analyze a wide range of data, including transaction history, account activity, and user behavior, to identify potential fraud.

For instance, banks can deploy machine learning-based fraud detection systems that examine the velocity of transactions, geographic anomalies, or unusual spending patterns.

When the system detects suspicious activity, it can trigger alerts or block transactions until further investigation is conducted.

In summary, leveraging machine learning for threat detection is a game-changer in the field of cybersecurity.

Machine learning offers the capability to detect malware, identify network anomalies, analyze user behavior, enhance email security, and automate incident response.

By applying machine learning techniques to various aspects of cybersecurity, organizations can improve their ability to detect and respond to threats, ultimately strengthening their overall security posture.

BOOK 3
TROJAN EXPOSED
EXPERT STRATEGIES FOR CYBER RESILIENCE

ROB BOTWRIGHT

Chapter 1: Understanding Advanced Trojan Tactics

Trojans are malicious software programs that disguise themselves as legitimate software, making them difficult to detect.

To evade detection, Trojans employ various techniques and tactics designed to bypass security measures and infiltrate target systems.

One common Trojan evasion technique is the use of encryption to obfuscate the payload.

By encrypting the payload, the Trojan conceals its true nature, making it appear as harmless data.

To decrypt and execute the payload, the Trojan uses a decryption routine that is often embedded within the malicious code.

This technique prevents security solutions from identifying the payload as malicious until it is decrypted and executed, allowing the Trojan to bypass initial security checks.

To deploy this evasion technique, a Trojan creator can use encryption libraries or algorithms within the code to encrypt the payload and then include the decryption routine.

Once the Trojan is executed on the target system, it can use the decryption routine to unlock and execute its malicious payload.

Another Trojan evasion technique involves the use of polymorphism, where the Trojan continuously modifies its code to create unique variants.

Polymorphic Trojans change their code structure with each infection, altering their appearance and behavior while maintaining their core malicious functionality.

This dynamic behavior makes it challenging for antivirus and intrusion detection systems to detect and block the Trojan.

To implement polymorphism, the Trojan's code must include a polymorphic engine that generates random or semi-random variations of the code.

The Trojan creator can employ various techniques, such as code obfuscation, instruction reordering, or adding meaningless instructions, to create these variations.

When executed, the Trojan's polymorphic engine generates a new, unique version of the malware, making it difficult for signature-based detection methods to identify the threat.

Trojans can also employ evasion techniques related to their command-and-control (C&C) communication.

C&C servers serve as a central control point for Trojans, allowing attackers to remotely manage and control infected systems.

To evade detection, Trojans may use techniques like domain generation algorithms (DGAs) or domain fluxing to dynamically change the domain names and IP addresses they use to communicate with the C&C server.

DGAs generate a large number of potential domain names based on a predefined algorithm and a seed value.

The Trojan periodically calculates a domain name from the algorithm and attempts to connect to it.

By constantly changing the domain names, Trojans make it difficult for security solutions to identify and block C&C communication.

To employ this evasion technique, a Trojan creator embeds the DGA algorithm and a seed value within the malware code.

The Trojan then periodically generates domain names and attempts to establish connections to the C&C server using these domains.

Another Trojan evasion technique is process injection, where the Trojan injects its malicious code into the memory space of a legitimate process running on the target system.

By doing this, the Trojan camouflages itself as part of a trusted process, making it harder to detect and remove.

Process injection can occur through various methods, such as code injection, thread injection, or process hollowing.

For example, a Trojan may use code injection to insert its malicious code into a running process like svchost.exe.

This allows the Trojan to execute its code within the context of a legitimate process, making it less conspicuous and evading detection by security solutions.

To employ process injection, the Trojan's code must include the necessary routines and techniques to identify and inject its payload into a target process.

These routines often use operating system functions and APIs to manipulate the target process's memory space.

Another evasion technique involves Trojan creators using steganography to hide malicious code within seemingly innocuous files or data.

Steganography is the practice of concealing information within other data to avoid detection.

Trojans may hide their payload within image files, documents, or even audio files.

By embedding the malicious code in this way, the Trojan appears benign and can bypass security checks.

To deploy steganography, Trojan creators encode their payload within a carrier file using specific algorithms.

The carrier file could be an image in which the payload is encoded in the least significant bits of the pixel values.

To execute the payload, the Trojan decodes it from the carrier file and then executes it within the target system.

Trojans can also employ self-modifying code techniques to evade detection.

Self-modifying code is code that can change its own instructions or behavior during runtime.

By continuously modifying its code, the Trojan can avoid static analysis techniques used by security solutions.

To implement self-modifying code, the Trojan includes routines that dynamically alter its instructions or behavior.

These routines often use assembly language or machine code to manipulate the Trojan's code sections.

By modifying its code during execution, the Trojan remains elusive and difficult to detect through static analysis.

In summary, Trojans use a variety of evasion techniques to bypass security measures and infiltrate target systems.

These techniques include encryption, polymorphism, dynamic C&C communication, process injection, steganography, and self-modifying code.

Understanding these evasion tactics is crucial for cybersecurity professionals to develop effective strategies for detecting and mitigating Trojan infections.

Covert communication channels are a crucial aspect of cybersecurity, as they play a significant role in the realm of cyber espionage, data exfiltration, and stealthy communication between malicious actors and compromised systems.

These channels enable malicious entities to transmit information surreptitiously, avoiding detection by security systems and remaining under the radar.

One common covert communication technique is the use of covert channels within network protocols, which allow hidden data transfer within the normal traffic of legitimate network communication.

For instance, a covert channel can be established by encoding data within seemingly innocent network packets, such as the timing of packet transmissions, specific combinations of flags, or variations in packet sizes.

To deploy this technique, a malicious actor can use tools or scripts to manipulate network traffic, embedding hidden messages within the packets.

These messages can then be extracted on the receiving end through the analysis of the covert channel.

Another covert communication method involves exploiting unused or less-monitored communication paths within a network, such as unused ports or protocols, to transmit data covertly.

Malicious actors can utilize these overlooked avenues to establish covert channels, ensuring that their activities go unnoticed.

For example, a hacker could use a well-known port, such as Port 80, typically associated with web traffic, to send and receive data that mimics legitimate web traffic, making it difficult for security systems to differentiate between normal and covert communication.

To implement this technique, the malicious actor must configure their tools or malware to communicate through these alternative channels, often requiring specific port configurations and encryption methods.

Covert communication channels can also be established through DNS (Domain Name System) traffic, exploiting the DNS protocol's characteristics to hide data transfer.

One method involves encoding data within subdomains or queries sent to a DNS server.

For example, a malicious actor might create a subdomain with a specific name that represents a letter or number, encoding information as a sequence of subdomains.

To send data, the malware generates DNS queries for these subdomains, and on the receiving end, the covert data is extracted by analyzing the DNS logs.

Implementing this technique involves configuring the malware to generate specific DNS queries and encode the data in a format that can be decoded later.

Another covert communication approach exploits the use of social media platforms and messaging services for clandestine communication.

Malicious actors create seemingly benign accounts and post seemingly innocuous content, but within the content lies hidden messages, often using steganography techniques.

Steganography involves concealing data within media files, such as images or audio files, by subtly altering the file's binary code.

To transmit covert messages through social media, a hacker can upload images containing hidden data to their account.

The recipient can then download these images and extract the concealed information using steganography tools.

Deploying this technique requires the use of steganography software to embed data within images, ensuring that the modifications are imperceptible to the human eye.

Covert channels can also be established using legitimate communication protocols, such as email services.

Hackers can employ these channels to send hidden data within email attachments or message headers.

For example, an attacker might encode sensitive information within the metadata of an image attached to an email. The recipient can then decode the hidden data from the image's metadata.

To employ this technique, the malicious actor must use appropriate encoding methods and ensure that the modifications to the email content remain unnoticeable. Covert communication channels also extend to offline methods, such as the use of physical devices and techniques to transmit data surreptitiously.

One example is the use of "dead drops," where physical storage devices, like USB drives or SD cards, are strategically placed in physical locations.

These storage devices contain hidden data, and individuals with knowledge of the location can retrieve them.

To establish a dead drop, a malicious actor must physically place the storage device in a discreet location and share the location details with the intended recipient.

Covert channels can even be created within the electromagnetic spectrum, exploiting radio frequencies to transmit data.

This technique, known as "covert radio communication," involves encoding data into electromagnetic signals.

Malicious actors can use radio waves to communicate between devices, with the data encoded in the frequency or amplitude variations of the signal.

To implement covert radio communication, a hacker would require specialized hardware and knowledge of radio frequency encoding techniques.

In summary, covert communication channels are a critical component of cyber espionage and covert operations, allowing malicious actors to hide their activities and exchange information stealthily.

These channels encompass a wide range of techniques, including covert network protocols, unused communication paths, DNS traffic, social media, email, physical storage devices, and radio communication.

Understanding these covert communication methods is essential for cybersecurity professionals to detect and mitigate covert data exfiltration and unauthorized communication within networks and systems.

Chapter 2: Cyber Resilience: A Holistic Approach

Cyber resilience is a fundamental concept in modern cybersecurity, addressing the need for organizations to not only defend against cyber threats but also to effectively respond and recover from them.

In today's digital landscape, cyberattacks have become increasingly sophisticated and frequent, posing significant risks to organizations' operations, reputation, and sensitive data.

Traditional cybersecurity measures, while essential, are no longer sufficient on their own to protect against the evolving threat landscape.

Cyber resilience encompasses a broader and more proactive approach to cybersecurity, emphasizing the organization's ability to adapt and continue its operations even in the face of cyber incidents.

One key aspect of cyber resilience is the recognition that cyberattacks are not a matter of "if" but "when."

Organizations must assume that they will face cyber incidents at some point and prepare accordingly.

This proactive mindset is crucial in building cyber resilience.

To deploy this approach, organizations can implement incident response plans that outline the steps to be taken in the event of a cyber incident.

These plans should include clear roles and responsibilities, communication strategies, and technical procedures for detecting, mitigating, and recovering from incidents.

Cyber resilience also emphasizes the importance of robust backup and disaster recovery strategies.

Organizations should regularly back up their critical data and systems to ensure that they can recover quickly and effectively in the event of data breaches, ransomware attacks, or other cyber incidents.

To implement this, organizations can use backup solutions that automate the backup process and provide redundancy in case of data loss.

Additionally, organizations should regularly test their backup and recovery procedures to ensure their effectiveness.

Another key aspect of cyber resilience is threat intelligence and proactive threat hunting.

Instead of waiting for threats to manifest themselves, organizations can actively seek out signs of potential threats and vulnerabilities within their networks.

To deploy this approach, organizations can use threat intelligence feeds and security information and event management (SIEM) systems to monitor their networks for suspicious activities and indicators of compromise.

Furthermore, organizations can employ threat hunting teams or services that proactively search for signs of malicious activity within their environments.

Cyber resilience also involves a focus on employee awareness and training.

Human error remains one of the leading causes of cyber incidents, with employees inadvertently clicking on phishing emails, downloading malicious attachments, or falling victim to social engineering attacks.

To address this, organizations can provide comprehensive cybersecurity training and awareness programs for their employees.

These programs should educate employees about the latest cyber threats, safe online practices, and how to recognize and report suspicious activities.

To deploy this, organizations can use e-learning platforms, conduct regular cybersecurity workshops, and provide ongoing training materials and resources.

Furthermore, organizations can implement robust access control and authentication mechanisms to limit unauthorized access to their systems and data.

Implementing strong password policies, multi-factor authentication (MFA), and privileged access management (PAM) solutions can significantly enhance cyber resilience.

To deploy this, organizations can use access management tools that provide centralized control over user access and authentication processes.

Additionally, organizations should regularly review and update their access control policies to ensure they align with evolving cybersecurity best practices.

Cyber resilience also involves a focus on continuous monitoring and security assessments.

Organizations should continuously monitor their networks and systems for vulnerabilities and potential security weaknesses.

This includes regularly conducting penetration testing, vulnerability scanning, and security assessments.

To deploy this, organizations can use vulnerability scanning tools to identify weaknesses in their systems and networks.

Additionally, they can hire ethical hackers to conduct penetration tests to identify potential vulnerabilities that malicious actors could exploit.

Moreover, organizations should prioritize the use of security patches and updates to keep their systems and software up to date.

Unpatched vulnerabilities are a common target for cyberattacks, and organizations must promptly apply security patches to mitigate these risks.

To deploy this, organizations can use automated patch management solutions that streamline the patching process and ensure that critical updates are applied promptly.

Furthermore, organizations should have a clear incident response plan in place to handle cyber incidents effectively.

This plan should outline the steps to be taken in the event of an incident, including communication protocols, technical procedures, and reporting mechanisms.

To deploy this, organizations can establish an incident response team that is well-trained and equipped to handle a range of cyber incidents.

Additionally, they should conduct regular tabletop exercises and simulations to test the effectiveness of their incident response plan.

Cyber resilience also emphasizes the importance of collaboration and information sharing within the cybersecurity community.

Organizations can benefit from sharing threat intelligence, best practices, and lessons learned with other organizations and industry groups.

To deploy this, organizations can participate in threat information sharing platforms and industry-specific cybersecurity associations.

Collaboration and information sharing can help organizations stay ahead of emerging threats and vulnerabilities.

In summary, cyber resilience is a vital component of modern cybersecurity, focusing on an organization's ability to adapt, respond, and recover from cyber incidents.

It involves proactive measures such as incident response planning, robust backup and recovery strategies, threat intelligence, employee training, access control, continuous monitoring, and collaboration with the cybersecurity community.

By adopting a cyber-resilient mindset and implementing these strategies, organizations can better protect themselves against the ever-evolving landscape of cyber threats.

Integrating resilience into the organizational culture is essential in ensuring that cybersecurity is not just a set of practices and technologies but a mindset that permeates the entire organization.

To achieve this, it is crucial to foster a culture of cybersecurity awareness and responsibility from the top down, starting with leadership and extending to all employees.

Leaders within the organization must set the tone for cybersecurity resilience by demonstrating a commitment to its importance and by actively participating in cybersecurity initiatives.

This can be achieved through visible support for cybersecurity programs, regular communication about the significance of cybersecurity, and a dedication to allocating resources for its implementation.

Leaders must understand that cybersecurity is not solely an IT issue but a business imperative that impacts the organization's overall success and reputation.

To integrate resilience into the organizational culture, leaders should also prioritize cybersecurity training and awareness programs for all employees.

These programs should not be viewed as one-time events but as ongoing efforts to keep employees informed about the latest cyber threats, safe online practices, and the organization's cybersecurity policies and procedures.

Leaders can lead by example by participating in these training programs and reinforcing their importance.

Furthermore, organizations should create clear and comprehensive cybersecurity policies and procedures that are easily accessible to all employees.

These policies should outline expected behaviors, responsibilities, and consequences for non-compliance.

Having well-defined policies helps set clear expectations and reinforces the importance of cybersecurity within the organization.

Leaders can enforce these policies consistently and communicate their significance to employees.

To deploy this, organizations can establish a centralized repository or intranet where employees can access and review cybersecurity policies and procedures.

Additionally, organizations can implement regular cybersecurity audits and assessments to ensure that employees are complying with established policies.

It is also essential to encourage a culture of open communication and reporting when it comes to potential security incidents or breaches.

Employees should feel comfortable reporting any suspicious activities or security concerns without fear of reprisal.

Leaders can create this environment of trust by emphasizing the importance of early detection and swift response to security incidents.

To deploy this, organizations can establish anonymous reporting channels or incident response teams that are dedicated to handling security concerns.

Leaders should actively promote these reporting mechanisms and ensure that employees are aware of their existence.

Another crucial aspect of integrating resilience into the organizational culture is to promote a sense of collective responsibility.

Every employee, regardless of their role, plays a part in the organization's cybersecurity posture.

Leaders should emphasize that cybersecurity is a team effort and that everyone has a role to play in protecting the organization.

To deploy this, organizations can conduct regular cybersecurity drills and simulations that involve employees from different departments.

These exercises can help employees understand their roles and responsibilities during a security incident and reinforce the concept of collective responsibility.

Furthermore, organizations should recognize and reward cybersecurity awareness and best practices.

Leaders can create incentives for employees who demonstrate a strong commitment to cybersecurity, such as acknowledgment in company newsletters or rewards programs. Positive reinforcement can motivate employees to actively engage in cybersecurity efforts.

To deploy this, organizations can establish recognition programs or incorporate cybersecurity performance metrics into employee evaluations.

Additionally, organizations should continuously educate their workforce about emerging cybersecurity threats and best practices.

Cybersecurity is an ever-evolving field, and employees must stay informed about the latest developments to remain resilient against new threats.

Leaders can promote ongoing learning by providing access to cybersecurity resources, training, and certifications.

To deploy this, organizations can invest in cybersecurity training platforms and encourage employees to pursue relevant certifications.

Leaders should also foster collaboration among different departments within the organization.

Cybersecurity is not solely the responsibility of the IT department; it involves all areas of the organization.

Leaders can encourage cross-functional collaboration by facilitating regular meetings or working groups that include representatives from various departments.

These forums can provide a platform for discussing cybersecurity challenges and sharing insights.

To deploy this, organizations can establish cross-functional cybersecurity committees or task forces to address specific security issues.

Furthermore, leaders should emphasize the importance of incident response planning and readiness.

Organizations should have well-defined incident response plans in place and regularly conduct drills to ensure that employees know how to respond effectively to security incidents.

Leaders can instill confidence in the organization's incident response capabilities by actively participating in these exercises and demonstrating a commitment to rapid recovery.

To deploy this, organizations can establish incident response teams and conduct tabletop exercises to simulate real-world scenarios.

Finally, leaders must lead by example when it comes to cybersecurity hygiene.

Leaders should practice what they preach by following best practices, such as strong password management, regular software updates, and safe online behavior.

When employees see their leaders prioritizing cybersecurity, they are more likely to do the same.

To deploy this, leaders should adhere to cybersecurity policies and actively participate in security awareness programs and training.

In summary, integrating resilience into the organizational culture is a multifaceted effort that requires commitment from leadership and active engagement from all employees.

Leaders must set the tone by demonstrating their dedication to cybersecurity, prioritizing training and awareness, and enforcing policies consistently.

By fostering a culture of trust, collective responsibility, ongoing learning, and collaboration, organizations can build a resilient cybersecurity culture that is adaptable and prepared to face evolving threats.

Chapter 3: Threat Intelligence and Proactive Defense

Gathering actionable threat intelligence is a critical component of modern cybersecurity strategies, as it provides organizations with valuable insights into the evolving threat landscape.

This intelligence empowers organizations to make informed decisions and take proactive measures to protect their systems and data.

One of the primary sources of threat intelligence is external feeds from reputable cybersecurity organizations and government agencies.

These feeds provide information about known threats, vulnerabilities, and indicators of compromise (IoCs) that can help organizations identify and respond to potential threats.

To deploy this, organizations can subscribe to threat intelligence feeds and integrate them into their security information and event management (SIEM) systems.

Additionally, organizations can leverage open-source threat intelligence sharing platforms, such as the Open Threat Exchange (OTX), to access and contribute to threat intelligence.

Another valuable source of threat intelligence is internal data generated within the organization.

This includes logs, network traffic data, and incident reports that can provide insights into potential security incidents and vulnerabilities.

To deploy this, organizations can implement robust logging and monitoring solutions that capture and analyze data from their networks, systems, and applications.

Furthermore, organizations can establish an incident response team responsible for investigating and documenting security incidents to gather actionable intelligence.

Social media platforms and forums can also serve as sources of threat intelligence.

Malicious actors often discuss their activities on these platforms, providing clues and insights into their tactics, techniques, and procedures (TTPs).

To deploy this, organizations can assign personnel to monitor relevant social media channels and forums for mentions of their organization, industry, or related keywords.

Additionally, organizations can leverage threat intelligence platforms that collect and analyze data from social media and other online sources.

Vulnerability databases and security bulletins are crucial sources of threat intelligence, as they provide information about newly discovered vulnerabilities and patches.

To deploy this, organizations can subscribe to vulnerability databases and security mailing lists relevant to their technologies and applications.

Moreover, organizations should establish a patch management process that prioritizes the timely deployment of security updates and patches.

Dark web monitoring is another valuable source of threat intelligence.

The dark web is a hidden part of the internet where illegal activities often occur, including the sale of stolen data, hacking tools, and malware.

To deploy this, organizations can utilize dark web monitoring services that continuously search for mentions of their organization, leaked data, or other relevant information.

Additionally, organizations can collaborate with law enforcement agencies to investigate and mitigate threats originating from the dark web.

Collaboration with industry peers and Information Sharing and Analysis Centers (ISACs) is essential for gathering actionable threat intelligence.

Sharing information about threats and vulnerabilities within a trusted community allows organizations to benefit from collective insights and experiences.

To deploy this, organizations can join relevant ISACs or industry-specific information sharing groups.

Moreover, organizations can establish partnerships with trusted peers for threat intelligence sharing.

Machine learning and artificial intelligence (AI) technologies can enhance the process of gathering actionable threat intelligence.

These technologies can analyze large volumes of data quickly and identify patterns, anomalies, and potential threats that may be missed by manual analysis.

To deploy this, organizations can implement machine learning algorithms and AI-driven threat detection systems within their cybersecurity infrastructure.

Furthermore, organizations should regularly review and update their threat intelligence feeds and sources.

The threat landscape is dynamic, and threat actors constantly adapt their tactics.

To stay ahead, organizations should ensure that their threat intelligence sources remain relevant and up to date.

To deploy this, organizations can establish a continuous monitoring and evaluation process for their threat intelligence sources.

Additionally, organizations should foster a culture of information sharing and collaboration among their cybersecurity teams.

Cross-functional teams that include security analysts, incident responders, and threat intelligence analysts can work together to gather, analyze, and act on threat intelligence effectively.

To deploy this, organizations can conduct regular training and workshops that promote collaboration and information sharing among different cybersecurity functions.

Moreover, organizations should prioritize the dissemination of actionable threat intelligence to relevant stakeholders.

Effective communication ensures that security teams, IT departments, and business leaders have access to timely and relevant threat intelligence.

To deploy this, organizations can establish clear communication channels and protocols for sharing threat intelligence.

Furthermore, organizations can develop tailored threat intelligence reports and alerts for different audiences, highlighting the potential impact and recommended actions.

In summary, gathering actionable threat intelligence is a foundational element of a robust cybersecurity strategy.

Organizations must leverage a combination of external feeds, internal data, social media monitoring, vulnerability databases, dark web monitoring, collaboration with peers, machine learning, and effective communication to stay informed and resilient in the face of evolving cyber threats.

By continuously refining their threat intelligence sources and fostering a culture of collaboration, organizations can enhance their ability to detect and respond to threats effectively.

Chapter 4: Advanced Security Architecture and Design

Secure cloud architecture is a fundamental consideration for organizations as they increasingly migrate their workloads and data to cloud environments.

Cloud computing offers numerous benefits, including scalability, flexibility, and cost-efficiency, but it also introduces unique security challenges that must be addressed.

One of the first steps in achieving a secure cloud architecture is selecting a reputable and security-focused cloud service provider (CSP).

Organizations should assess CSPs based on their security certifications, compliance with industry standards, and the availability of security features such as encryption, identity and access management, and intrusion detection.

To deploy this, organizations can conduct a thorough evaluation of CSPs and choose one that aligns with their security requirements and regulatory obligations.

Once a CSP is selected, organizations should adopt a shared responsibility model for security.

In this model, both the CSP and the customer have specific security responsibilities.

The CSP typically manages the security of the cloud infrastructure, while the customer is responsible for securing their data and applications within the cloud.

To deploy this, organizations should clearly define their security responsibilities and establish a security framework that covers both the CSP's and the customer's roles.

Encryption is a critical component of secure cloud architecture.

Data should be encrypted both in transit and at rest to protect it from unauthorized access.

To deploy this, organizations can implement encryption protocols such as TLS/SSL for data in transit and use encryption keys to secure data at rest.

Furthermore, organizations should consider using hardware security modules (HSMs) for key management to enhance the security of encryption keys.

Identity and access management (IAM) is another essential aspect of secure cloud architecture.

Organizations should implement strong authentication mechanisms, such as multi-factor authentication (MFA), and enforce strict access controls to ensure that only authorized users have access to cloud resources.

To deploy this, organizations can use IAM solutions provided by the CSP or deploy third-party IAM solutions that integrate with the cloud environment.

Network security is a critical consideration in secure cloud architecture.

Organizations should establish network segmentation and implement firewalls and intrusion detection systems (IDS) to monitor and protect traffic within the cloud environment.

To deploy this, organizations can configure network security groups and virtual private clouds (VPCs) to isolate resources and control traffic flow.

Regularly monitoring and auditing cloud resources and configurations is essential to maintaining a secure cloud architecture.

Organizations should use cloud-native security tools and third-party solutions to continuously monitor for security incidents and vulnerabilities.

To deploy this, organizations can set up automated monitoring and alerting systems that provide real-time visibility into their cloud environment.

Incident response and disaster recovery plans are crucial components of secure cloud architecture.

Organizations should have well-defined procedures for responding to security incidents and data breaches, as well as backup and recovery strategies to ensure business continuity.

To deploy this, organizations can establish an incident response team and regularly test their disaster recovery plans.

Compliance with industry-specific regulations and standards is a top priority for many organizations.

Secure cloud architecture should include mechanisms for meeting compliance requirements, such as data encryption, access controls, and audit trails.

To deploy this, organizations can work with their CSP to ensure that their cloud environment complies with relevant regulations and standards.

Security awareness and training programs are essential to ensure that employees are knowledgeable about secure cloud practices.

Organizations should educate their staff about cloud security risks and best practices, such as secure data sharing and password management.

To deploy this, organizations can provide cybersecurity training modules and conduct regular awareness campaigns.

Security automation and orchestration are valuable tools in secure cloud architecture.

Organizations can use automation to enforce security policies, detect and respond to threats, and streamline security operations.

To deploy this, organizations can implement security automation tools that integrate with their cloud environment.

Logging and auditing are critical for maintaining visibility into cloud activities and detecting security incidents.

Organizations should configure logging and auditing features provided by the CSP and retain logs for an appropriate period.

To deploy this, organizations can set up centralized log management and analysis tools to review and analyze log data.

Regular security assessments and penetration testing are essential for evaluating the effectiveness of security controls in a cloud environment.

Organizations should conduct vulnerability assessments and penetration tests to identify and remediate weaknesses.

To deploy this, organizations can engage third-party security firms or use cloud-native security testing tools.

Secure DevOps practices should be integrated into the development and deployment processes within a secure cloud architecture.

Organizations should ensure that security is considered throughout the software development lifecycle, from design to deployment.

To deploy this, organizations can adopt DevSecOps principles and incorporate security testing and scanning tools into their DevOps pipelines.

Data governance and classification play a crucial role in secure cloud architecture.

Organizations should classify data based on its sensitivity and implement appropriate access controls and data protection measures.

To deploy this, organizations can use data classification tools and establish data governance policies.

In summary, achieving a secure cloud architecture requires a multi-faceted approach that includes selecting a reputable CSP, implementing encryption and strong authentication, managing identities and access, securing the network, monitoring and auditing, incident response and disaster recovery planning, compliance, training, automation, logging and auditing, security assessments, DevSecOps practices, data governance, and classification.

By addressing each of these components, organizations can create a robust and resilient cloud environment that protects against evolving security threats.

Microsegmentation is a network security strategy that divides a network into smaller, isolated segments to enhance security.

This approach allows organizations to control and monitor traffic between different segments and limit the lateral movement of attackers within their network.

Microsegmentation can be implemented using various technologies and tools, and it plays a critical role in modern network security.

One of the primary benefits of microsegmentation is that it reduces the attack surface by isolating different parts of the network.

This means that even if an attacker gains access to one segment, they will have limited visibility and access to other parts of the network.

To deploy microsegmentation, organizations can use network segmentation tools and technologies that provide granular control over traffic flows.

For example, software-defined networking (SDN) solutions allow organizations to create and manage network segments dynamically.

In a typical microsegmentation setup, network segments are created based on specific criteria, such as the type of application or the sensitivity of the data being accessed.

Once segments are defined, organizations can implement access controls and firewall rules to restrict traffic between them.

To deploy this, organizations can use SDN controllers and switches that support microsegmentation policies.

Furthermore, organizations can implement microsegmentation at various network levels, including at the data center, cloud environment, and even on endpoint devices.

Microsegmentation can help organizations protect critical assets and data by isolating them from less secure parts of the network.

For example, in a data center environment, organizations can create separate segments for web servers, application servers, and database servers.

By doing so, they can enforce strict access controls and firewall rules to prevent unauthorized access and lateral movement.

To deploy this, organizations can use virtualization and cloud security solutions that support microsegmentation policies.

Moreover, organizations can leverage identity-based microsegmentation, which focuses on user and device identities rather than just IP addresses.

This approach allows organizations to create security policies based on user roles and device attributes, providing more granular control over network access.

To deploy this, organizations can integrate identity and access management (IAM) solutions with their microsegmentation strategy.

Another advantage of microsegmentation is its ability to enhance threat detection and response.

By isolating network segments, organizations can monitor traffic more effectively and detect anomalous or suspicious behavior.

For example, if a user or device in one segment starts communicating with a segment it shouldn't, it can trigger alerts and automated responses.

To deploy this, organizations can use network monitoring and security analytics tools that integrate with their microsegmentation framework.

Additionally, organizations can implement microsegmentation as part of a zero-trust security strategy.

Zero trust assumes that no user or device should be trusted by default, even if they are inside the corporate network.

Microsegmentation plays a critical role in enforcing this principle by isolating and controlling network traffic regardless of where it originates.

To deploy this, organizations can adopt a zero-trust framework and incorporate microsegmentation policies into their network architecture.

One of the challenges of microsegmentation is managing and maintaining the policies and rules that govern network segments.

As organizations create more segments and define complex access controls, the management of microsegmentation policies can become cumbersome.

To address this challenge, organizations can use network security policy management tools that provide a centralized view and automation capabilities.

Moreover, organizations should regularly review and update their microsegmentation policies to ensure they align with changing business requirements and security threats.

Another consideration in microsegmentation is ensuring that it does not introduce performance bottlenecks or network latency.

When implementing microsegmentation, organizations should carefully design their network architecture and consider the potential impact on network performance.

To mitigate performance issues, organizations can use high-performance networking hardware and consider offloading security functions to dedicated appliances or virtual machines.

Furthermore, organizations should conduct thorough testing and performance monitoring to identify and address any bottlenecks.

Microsegmentation is not a one-time project but an ongoing security strategy that requires continuous monitoring and adaptation.

As organizations evolve and their network requirements change, microsegmentation policies should be adjusted accordingly.

To maintain the effectiveness of microsegmentation, organizations should conduct regular security assessments and penetration testing to identify and remediate weaknesses.

Additionally, organizations should keep abreast of emerging threats and vulnerabilities that may require updates to their microsegmentation policies.

In summary, microsegmentation is a powerful network security strategy that provides granular control over traffic flows, enhances threat detection and response, and supports a zero-trust security model.

By carefully planning, deploying, and managing microsegmentation policies, organizations can strengthen their network security and protect critical assets and data from cyber threats.

Chapter 5: Zero Trust Frameworks and Identity Management

Implementing Zero Trust principles is a transformative approach to cybersecurity that challenges traditional network security models.

Zero Trust is based on the premise that organizations should not automatically trust any user or device, even if they are inside the corporate network.

Instead, trust is verified continuously through strong authentication, access controls, and monitoring.

To deploy Zero Trust principles effectively, organizations need to adopt a holistic strategy that encompasses people, devices, applications, and data.

One of the foundational elements of Zero Trust is identity and access management (IAM).

Organizations should establish strong authentication mechanisms, such as multi-factor authentication (MFA), to verify the identity of users and devices.

To deploy this, organizations can implement IAM solutions that support MFA and integrate them with their existing identity providers.

Furthermore, organizations should use identity as the basis for access controls and policies.

Access to resources should be granted on a least-privileged basis, meaning users and devices are only given access to the resources necessary to perform their tasks.

To deploy this, organizations can define access control policies that are tied to specific user roles and device attributes.

Another key component of Zero Trust is network segmentation.

Traditional network perimeters are porous, and attackers can move laterally once they gain access.

Zero Trust advocates for the segmentation of networks into smaller, isolated segments that are protected by access controls.

To deploy this, organizations can use network segmentation tools and technologies, such as software-defined networking (SDN) and microsegmentation.

Moreover, organizations should encrypt data both in transit and at rest to protect it from unauthorized access.

Encryption ensures that even if data is intercepted or stolen, it remains unreadable without the appropriate decryption keys.

To deploy this, organizations can implement encryption protocols, such as Transport Layer Security (TLS) for data in transit and encryption solutions for data at rest.

Monitoring and continuous verification are essential in a Zero Trust model.

Organizations should continuously monitor user and device behavior to detect anomalous or suspicious activity.

To deploy this, organizations can use security information and event management (SIEM) systems and user and entity behavior analytics (UEBA) tools.

Additionally, organizations should establish automated alerting and response mechanisms to react swiftly to potential security incidents.

A key principle of Zero Trust is the concept of "never trust, always verify."

This means that organizations should verify the trustworthiness of every user, device, and transaction, regardless of their location or network.

To deploy this, organizations can implement continuous authentication mechanisms, such as adaptive authentication, which evaluates the risk associated with each access attempt.

Moreover, organizations should adopt a "zero-trust network access" (ZTNA) approach.

In ZTNA, users and devices are granted access to specific applications based on their identity and the trustworthiness of their connections. To deploy this, organizations can use ZTNA solutions that provide secure and granular access controls.

Endpoint security is a critical aspect of Zero Trust.

Organizations should ensure that devices connecting to the network are secure and comply with security policies.

To deploy this, organizations can use endpoint detection and response (EDR) solutions to monitor and enforce security on endpoints. Furthermore, organizations should implement secure device management practices, including regular patching and updates. Data protection is paramount in a Zero Trust model. Organizations should classify data based on its sensitivity and apply appropriate protection measures.

To deploy this, organizations can use data classification tools and encryption technologies to safeguard sensitive data.

Moreover, organizations should implement data loss prevention (DLP) solutions to monitor and prevent the unauthorized sharing or leakage of sensitive information.

In a Zero Trust model, visibility is crucial.

Organizations should have a comprehensive view of their network, users, devices, and applications to make informed security decisions.

To deploy this, organizations can use network monitoring and visibility tools that provide real-time insights into network traffic and user activity.

Additionally, organizations should integrate threat intelligence feeds to stay informed about emerging threats and vulnerabilities.

Collaboration and communication are essential in a Zero Trust model.

Security teams, IT departments, and business units should work together to implement and enforce Zero Trust principles effectively.

To deploy this, organizations can establish cross-functional teams responsible for Zero Trust implementation and governance.

Moreover, organizations should promote a culture of security awareness and education among employees to ensure that everyone understands their role in maintaining a Zero Trust environment.

In summary, implementing Zero Trust principles is a proactive and forward-thinking approach to cybersecurity.

By adopting a holistic strategy that focuses on identity and access management, network segmentation, encryption, monitoring, continuous verification, endpoint security, data protection, visibility, collaboration, and communication, organizations can significantly enhance their security posture and protect against evolving threats.

Zero Trust is not a one-time project but an ongoing security philosophy that requires continuous monitoring, adaptation, and improvement to stay ahead of cyber adversaries.

Identity and Access Management (IAM) is a critical component of modern cybersecurity, and implementing best practices in this area is essential to protect an organization's sensitive data and resources.

IAM is the process of managing and controlling access to various systems, applications, and data within an organization, ensuring that only authorized users can access specific resources.

To deploy IAM best practices effectively, organizations need to follow a comprehensive approach that includes user authentication, access controls, and monitoring.

One of the fundamental principles of IAM is strong user authentication.

This involves ensuring that users prove their identity through multiple factors before gaining access to systems and data.

Organizations should implement multi-factor authentication (MFA) as a standard practice.

MFA requires users to provide two or more authentication factors, such as a password, a smart card, or a fingerprint, to access their accounts.

To deploy MFA, organizations can use IAM solutions that support MFA methods and integrate them into their existing authentication processes.

Moreover, organizations should enforce strong password policies.

This includes requiring users to create complex passwords that are difficult to guess and regularly updating them.

To deploy strong password policies, organizations can configure IAM systems to enforce password complexity rules and expiration periods.

Another critical aspect of IAM is access control.

Access control defines the permissions and privileges granted to users or systems based on their roles and responsibilities within the organization.

Organizations should follow the principle of least privilege, which means that users should only have access to the resources necessary to perform their job functions.

To deploy least privilege access, organizations can use IAM solutions to define and enforce access policies tied to specific user roles.

Furthermore, organizations should implement role-based access control (RBAC) to simplify access management.

RBAC assigns roles to users based on their job functions, and these roles dictate the level of access they have.

To deploy RBAC, organizations can use IAM systems to define roles and assign users to them accordingly.

Monitoring and auditing are crucial components of IAM best practices.

Organizations should continuously monitor user activity and access to detect unauthorized or suspicious behavior.

IAM systems can provide detailed logs and reports that help organizations track user actions and identify potential security threats.

To deploy monitoring and auditing, organizations can configure IAM solutions to generate logs and alerts for specific events, such as failed login attempts or changes to access permissions.

Moreover, organizations should establish automated alerting and response mechanisms to react promptly to security incidents.

IAM also involves privileged access management (PAM), which is the control and monitoring of privileged accounts.

Privileged accounts have elevated privileges and can access critical systems and data.

To deploy PAM, organizations can use specialized IAM solutions that manage and audit privileged accounts separately from regular user accounts.

Additionally, organizations should implement a strong onboarding and offboarding process for users.

When new employees join the organization, IAM systems should ensure that they receive the appropriate access permissions based on their roles.

Conversely, when employees leave or change roles, their access should be promptly revoked or modified to align with their new responsibilities.

IAM solutions can automate these processes to reduce the risk of human error.

Furthermore, organizations should regularly review and update access permissions to align with changing business requirements and security threats.

IAM systems can help automate access reviews and provide insights into user activity and access patterns.

IAM extends beyond the organization's internal network.

As organizations increasingly adopt cloud services and mobile devices, IAM best practices should be applied to these environments as well.

Cloud IAM solutions allow organizations to manage user identities and access policies across various cloud services and applications.

To deploy cloud IAM, organizations can use cloud identity providers and integrate them with their existing IAM infrastructure.

Mobile IAM solutions enable organizations to manage access to corporate resources from mobile devices securely.

To deploy mobile IAM, organizations can use mobile device management (MDM) solutions and mobile application management (MAM) solutions to enforce security policies and controls on mobile devices and applications.

Education and awareness are crucial components of IAM best practices.

Organizations should provide training and awareness programs to educate employees about the importance of IAM and security best practices.

Users should understand their role in maintaining the security of the organization's systems and data.

Moreover, organizations should promote a culture of security awareness and encourage employees to report any suspicious activity promptly.

In summary, Identity and Access Management is a foundational element of modern cybersecurity.

Implementing IAM best practices, including strong user authentication, access control, monitoring, auditing, privileged access management, onboarding and offboarding processes, regular access reviews, cloud IAM, mobile IAM, and education and awareness programs, helps organizations protect their data and resources effectively.

IAM is an ongoing process that requires continuous monitoring, adaptation, and improvement to keep up with evolving security threats and business needs.

Chapter 6: Secure Coding Practices and Software Development

The Secure Software Development Life Cycle (SDLC) is an essential framework for building secure software applications.

It is designed to integrate security into every phase of the software development process, reducing vulnerabilities and enhancing overall security.

The SDLC encompasses a series of stages, each with its security considerations and best practices.

One of the primary objectives of the Secure SDLC is to identify and mitigate security risks early in the development process.

To achieve this, organizations should start by defining security requirements during the planning phase.

Security requirements outline the security features, controls, and measures that the software application should have.

To deploy this, development teams can work closely with security experts to define and document security requirements.

Furthermore, organizations should conduct a comprehensive risk assessment during the planning phase to identify potential security threats and vulnerabilities.

A risk assessment helps prioritize security efforts and focus on the most critical areas.

To deploy this, organizations can use risk assessment methodologies and tools to evaluate the application's potential security risks.

In the design phase of the Secure SDLC, security architects should create a detailed security architecture that aligns with the security requirements.

This architecture should encompass security controls, encryption methods, and access controls.

To deploy this, organizations can use secure design principles and security patterns to create a robust security architecture.

Moreover, organizations should consider threat modeling during the design phase.

Threat modeling involves identifying potential threats and attack vectors that could target the application.

To deploy this, organizations can conduct threat modeling sessions with security experts to assess and mitigate security risks.

The implementation phase of the Secure SDLC involves writing code and building the software application.

During this phase, developers should follow secure coding practices and guidelines.

Secure coding practices help prevent common security vulnerabilities such as SQL injection, cross-site scripting (XSS), and buffer overflows.

To deploy this, organizations can provide developers with secure coding training and tools that scan code for vulnerabilities.

Additionally, organizations should conduct code reviews to identify and remediate security issues.

The testing phase is a critical part of the Secure SDLC.

It involves various types of testing, including functional testing, security testing, and vulnerability scanning.

Functional testing ensures that the software functions as intended, while security testing focuses on identifying security vulnerabilities.

To deploy this, organizations can use automated security testing tools and manual security testing techniques.

Furthermore, organizations should conduct penetration testing to simulate real-world attacks and assess the application's security posture.

Once the software application passes testing and is ready for deployment, organizations should consider a secure deployment strategy.

This involves configuring the production environment securely, applying security patches, and hardening the server and network configurations.

To deploy this, organizations can use deployment scripts and automation tools that enforce security configurations.

Moreover, organizations should implement continuous monitoring in the production environment to detect and respond to security incidents promptly.

The maintenance phase of the Secure SDLC involves ongoing monitoring, patch management, and incident response.

Organizations should have processes in place to monitor the application's security and performance continuously.

To deploy this, organizations can use security information and event management (SIEM) systems and intrusion detection systems (IDS) to monitor the production environment.

Furthermore, organizations should establish a patch management process to keep software components and libraries up to date.

Vulnerabilities in third-party libraries and components can pose security risks, so organizations should regularly review and update these dependencies.

To deploy this, organizations can use automated dependency scanning tools to identify and remediate vulnerabilities in third-party code.

Incident response planning is essential in case a security incident occurs.

Organizations should have an incident response team and a well-defined incident response plan in place.

To deploy this, organizations can conduct incident response drills and tabletop exercises to ensure that the team is prepared to respond effectively.

The Secure SDLC also emphasizes the importance of security awareness and training for development teams.

Educating developers about security best practices, common vulnerabilities, and secure coding techniques is essential.

To deploy this, organizations can provide security training programs and resources for development teams.

Furthermore, organizations should promote a culture of security awareness among all employees, emphasizing their role in maintaining the security of the software application.

In summary, the Secure Software Development Life Cycle (SDLC) is a comprehensive framework that integrates security into every phase of the software development process.

By following security best practices in planning, design, implementation, testing, deployment, maintenance, and incident response, organizations can build and maintain secure software applications that protect against security threats and vulnerabilities.

The Secure SDLC is an ongoing process that requires continuous improvement and adaptation to address evolving security challenges and business needs.

Code review and vulnerability assessment are essential practices in ensuring the security and reliability of software applications.

Code review involves a thorough examination of the source code by developers or security experts to identify issues, including security vulnerabilities, coding errors, and design flaws.

To perform a code review, developers can use tools like static analysis scanners or manually inspect the code line by line.

Static analysis tools, such as "Fortify" or "Checkmarx," automatically scan the code for known vulnerabilities and coding patterns that may lead to security issues.

To use a static analysis tool, developers typically integrate it into their development environment and configure it to analyze the code during the build process.

Manual code reviews, on the other hand, involve experienced developers or security professionals reviewing the code for issues that may not be detected by automated tools.

Developers can conduct code reviews collaboratively, using tools like "GitHub" or "Bitbucket," which provide code review features and allow multiple contributors to comment on code changes.

During a code review, developers should pay special attention to security-related issues such as input validation, output encoding, authentication, and authorization.

Input validation ensures that data provided by users or external systems is validated and sanitized to prevent security vulnerabilities like SQL injection and Cross-Site Scripting (XSS) attacks.

Developers can use functions like "htmlspecialchars" in PHP or "encodeURIComponent" in JavaScript to encode user inputs before using them in a web application.

Output encoding ensures that data displayed to users in web applications is correctly encoded to prevent XSS attacks.

Developers can use template engines like "Handlebars" or "Jinja" to automatically escape output data.

Authentication and authorization are crucial for ensuring that only authorized users can access certain functionalities or resources within an application.

Developers can implement authentication using libraries like "Passport.js" in Node.js or "Devise" in Ruby on Rails.

For authorization, developers can define roles and permissions using libraries like "CanCanCan" in Ruby on Rails or implement access control lists (ACLs) to control user access.

In addition to code review, vulnerability assessment is another critical aspect of securing software applications.

Vulnerability assessment involves using automated scanning tools and techniques to identify security weaknesses and vulnerabilities within an application or its infrastructure.

To perform a vulnerability assessment, organizations can use tools like "Nessus," "OpenVAS," or "Qualys" to scan for known vulnerabilities and configuration issues.

These tools provide reports detailing the vulnerabilities found and their severity, enabling organizations to prioritize and remediate them.

Vulnerability assessments should be conducted regularly, especially after code changes or updates to the software and its underlying infrastructure.

In addition to automated scanning tools, organizations should also perform manual penetration testing to identify vulnerabilities that automated tools may miss.

Penetration testing involves ethical hackers simulating real-world attacks to discover vulnerabilities and assess the overall security posture of the application.

To perform a penetration test, organizations can hire security professionals or penetration testing firms with expertise in the specific technology stack and architecture of the application.

Once vulnerabilities are identified through code review and vulnerability assessment, organizations should prioritize and remediate them.

Prioritization should consider the severity of the vulnerability, the potential impact on the application and its users, and the likelihood of exploitation.

Remediation may involve code changes, configuration adjustments, or software updates.

Developers can use version control systems like "Git" to manage code changes and track the progress of vulnerability remediation.

It is essential to keep software dependencies and libraries up to date, as vulnerabilities in third-party code can pose security risks.

Developers can use package managers like "npm" in Node.js or "Composer" in PHP to update dependencies regularly.

Furthermore, organizations should establish a vulnerability management process that includes patching vulnerabilities in a timely manner.

Patching involves applying security updates and fixes provided by software vendors or open-source projects.

Developers can use package managers or system update commands to apply patches to the operating system, web servers, databases, and other components of the application's infrastructure.

In addition to code review and vulnerability assessment, organizations should implement security controls and monitoring to detect and respond to security incidents.

Security controls may include intrusion detection systems (IDS), intrusion prevention systems (IPS), and web application firewalls (WAFs) to protect against threats.

Monitoring should involve continuous monitoring of logs, traffic, and system activity to identify suspicious or malicious behavior.

Security information and event management (SIEM) solutions can centralize and analyze logs from various sources to provide real-time insights into potential security threats.

In summary, code review and vulnerability assessment are crucial practices in the secure development of software applications.

By conducting code reviews, using automated scanning tools, and performing penetration testing, organizations can identify and remediate security vulnerabilities and weaknesses.

Additionally, prioritizing and regularly updating software dependencies, implementing security controls, and establishing monitoring and incident response processes are essential steps to maintain the security and reliability of software applications.

Chapter 7: Red and Blue Teaming for Resilience Testing

Red team simulation exercises are an essential component of modern cybersecurity practices, designed to evaluate an organization's security posture and resilience to real-world threats.

These exercises involve the creation of a simulated adversarial group, known as the red team, tasked with attempting to breach an organization's security defenses.

The primary objective of red teaming is to identify vulnerabilities, weaknesses, and blind spots in an organization's security measures.

Before initiating a red team exercise, it's crucial to define clear objectives and scope, including what assets, systems, or networks will be tested, and what types of attacks or scenarios the red team will simulate.

Once the scope is defined, the red team can begin its preparations, which may include researching the target organization, gathering intelligence, and developing attack strategies.

Red team members often have diverse skill sets, including penetration testing, social engineering, and advanced hacking techniques, allowing them to emulate a variety of threat actors.

To ensure the exercise is conducted safely and ethically, clear rules of engagement (ROE) must be established, outlining what actions are permissible and what boundaries must not be crossed.

To deploy this, organizations can develop a formal ROE document that is agreed upon by both the red team and the organization's security and legal teams.

Communication is a critical aspect of red team exercises, and it's important for the red team to maintain open channels of communication with the organization's security personnel.

This allows for real-time reporting of findings, potential security breaches, and any actions taken by the red team during the exercise.

For instance, red team members may use encrypted communication channels to report progress and findings while maintaining a level of secrecy required for the exercise.

Red team exercises can take on various forms, ranging from covert assessments where the organization's security team is unaware of the exercise's timing and objectives to more collaborative assessments where the red team works closely with the security team.

The choice of exercise format often depends on the organization's goals, resources, and the level of surprise and realism desired.

To deploy this, organizations can select the appropriate exercise format that aligns with their specific needs and goals.

In covert assessments, the red team attempts to breach the organization's defenses without any prior knowledge or coordination with the internal security team.

This format allows the organization to gauge its security team's ability to detect and respond to unexpected threats.

In contrast, collaborative assessments involve close coordination between the red team and the internal security team.

This format allows for a more controlled exercise where both teams can work together to identify vulnerabilities and weaknesses and develop effective countermeasures.

During a red team exercise, the red team may use various tactics and techniques to simulate real-world attacks.

These tactics can include phishing campaigns, exploiting software vulnerabilities, social engineering, and attempting to gain unauthorized access to critical systems.

To deploy this, organizations can specify the tactics and techniques that the red team is authorized to use in the exercise.

Phishing campaigns often involve sending deceptive emails to employees in an attempt to trick them into clicking on malicious links or downloading malware.

To simulate a phishing campaign, the red team may use email templates, social engineering techniques, and fake websites to lure employees into revealing sensitive information or compromising their systems.

Exploiting software vulnerabilities is another common tactic employed by red teams.

They may attempt to exploit known vulnerabilities in the organization's software or systems to gain unauthorized access or execute malicious code.

To deploy this, red teams can use penetration testing tools and techniques to identify and exploit vulnerabilities.

Social engineering is a tactic that relies on psychological manipulation to deceive individuals into divulging confidential information or performing actions that compromise security.

Red teams may use pretexting, baiting, or impersonation to exploit human vulnerabilities within the organization.

To deploy this, organizations can provide security awareness training to employees to recognize and resist social engineering attempts.

Gaining unauthorized access to critical systems is a core objective of red team exercises.

Red teams may attempt to breach the organization's network, servers, or applications to demonstrate the potential impact of a real cyberattack.

To deploy this, organizations can set up isolated environments or use virtualization technologies to ensure that the exercise does not disrupt production systems.

As the red team conducts its activities, the internal security team monitors and responds to the simulated threats.

This provides an opportunity to evaluate the organization's incident detection and response capabilities.

To deploy this, organizations can use security monitoring tools, intrusion detection systems (IDS), and security information and event management (SIEM) solutions to monitor the network and detect abnormal activities.

The organization's security team should also be prepared to respond to incidents promptly, investigate security alerts, and take appropriate actions to mitigate threats.

To deploy this, organizations can develop incident response plans and run tabletop exercises to ensure that the security team is well-prepared to handle security incidents.

Once the red team exercise is completed, a thorough debriefing and assessment are essential to analyze the findings and lessons learned.

The red team should provide a detailed report outlining the vulnerabilities and weaknesses discovered during the exercise and recommendations for improving security.

To deploy this, organizations can convene a debriefing session involving both the red team and the internal security team to discuss the exercise's outcomes and develop a roadmap for addressing the identified issues.

In summary, red team simulation exercises are valuable tools for evaluating an organization's security posture and resilience to real-world threats.

By defining clear objectives, establishing rules of engagement, and choosing the appropriate exercise format, organizations can gain insights into their vulnerabilities and weaknesses.

Additionally, by monitoring and responding to simulated threats, organizations can enhance their incident detection and response capabilities and develop effective countermeasures to protect against cyberattacks.

Blue team response and incident handling are critical components of an organization's cybersecurity strategy, focused on defending against and mitigating the impact of security incidents and breaches.

The blue team represents the defenders, consisting of internal security personnel responsible for protecting the organization's assets, networks, and data.

When an incident occurs, the blue team's primary objective is to detect, respond to, and recover from the incident while minimizing its impact.

To deploy this, organizations can establish a dedicated blue team responsible for incident response and recovery efforts.

Effective incident handling begins with the development of an incident response plan (IRP) that outlines the procedures and processes to follow when a security incident is detected.

The IRP should define roles and responsibilities within the blue team, specify communication channels, and establish incident classification and severity levels.

To deploy this, organizations can create and maintain an IRP document that is accessible to all relevant personnel and regularly updated to reflect changes in the organization's environment and threat landscape.

The blue team's incident detection capabilities are critical to identifying security incidents promptly.

Detection tools such as intrusion detection systems (IDS), intrusion prevention systems (IPS), and security information and event management (SIEM) solutions play a crucial role in monitoring network traffic, logs, and system activity for signs of suspicious or malicious behavior.

To deploy this, organizations can configure and maintain detection tools to generate alerts and notifications when abnormal activities or potential security threats are detected.

Additionally, organizations can use threat intelligence feeds to stay informed about emerging threats and vulnerabilities, enhancing their detection capabilities.

When a security incident is detected, the blue team must respond promptly and effectively to contain and mitigate the threat.

To deploy this, organizations can establish an incident response team (IRT) comprising individuals with specific roles and expertise, such as incident handlers, forensic analysts, and legal representatives.

Incident handlers play a pivotal role in responding to incidents by coordinating efforts, collecting and analyzing data, and making informed decisions to contain and mitigate the incident.

Forensic analysts are responsible for collecting and preserving evidence related to the incident, which may be crucial for legal and investigative purposes.

Legal representatives ensure that the organization complies with applicable laws and regulations during incident handling and may engage with law enforcement and legal authorities as necessary.

In addition to human resources, the blue team relies on a variety of tools and technologies to aid in incident response.

For example, digital forensics tools like "Autopsy" and "EnCase" can be used to analyze system and network artifacts to determine the extent of the incident and its impact.

To deploy this, organizations can provide their incident handlers and forensic analysts with access to the necessary tools and training.

Containment and eradication are critical phases of incident response, aimed at preventing further damage and eliminating the threat.

To deploy this, organizations can isolate affected systems or networks from the rest of the environment to prevent lateral movement by attackers.

Access control measures, such as disabling compromised accounts or changing passwords, can further restrict unauthorized access.

Once containment is achieved, the blue team can work to eradicate the root cause of the incident, such as identifying and removing malware or patching vulnerabilities.

The recovery phase of incident handling focuses on restoring affected systems and services to normal operations.

To deploy this, organizations can develop and maintain backups of critical data and systems to facilitate the recovery process.

Regularly testing and verifying the integrity of backups is essential to ensure their availability and reliability during incidents.

Furthermore, organizations can establish communication channels and procedures for notifying relevant stakeholders, including senior management, legal teams, and affected individuals, if required.

In some cases, organizations may be legally obligated to report certain types of incidents to regulatory authorities or affected individuals.

To deploy this, organizations should be aware of their legal and regulatory obligations and incorporate them into their incident response processes.

The post-incident phase involves conducting a thorough review and analysis of the incident response efforts to identify lessons learned and areas for improvement.

To deploy this, organizations can hold post-incident debriefings and assessments involving the incident response team to discuss what went well, what could have been done differently, and how to enhance future incident handling.

This phase also involves updating the incident response plan and implementing any necessary changes or improvements based on the lessons learned.

To deploy this, organizations should regularly review and update their IRP to ensure it remains effective in addressing evolving threats and vulnerabilities.

Effective communication is a crucial element of blue team response and incident handling.

To deploy this, organizations can establish clear lines of communication within the incident response team and with external parties, such as vendors, law enforcement agencies, and affected individuals.

Timely and accurate communication helps coordinate efforts, gather information, and facilitate a more effective response.

Additionally, organizations can engage with external organizations, such as industry-specific information sharing and analysis centers (ISACs) or computer emergency response teams (CERTs), to share threat intelligence and collaborate on incident response.

In summary, blue team response and incident handling are essential for organizations to effectively detect, respond to, and recover from security incidents and breaches.

By developing an incident response plan, establishing incident response teams, leveraging detection tools, and following best practices, organizations can enhance their ability to protect their assets and minimize the impact of security incidents.

Chapter 8: Security Compliance and Risk Management

Compliance frameworks and standards are crucial in the realm of cybersecurity and information technology, as they provide organizations with a structured approach to ensuring that they adhere to industry best practices and legal requirements.

These frameworks and standards serve as guidelines that help organizations establish and maintain effective security practices to protect their assets, data, and systems.

One widely recognized compliance framework is the NIST Cybersecurity Framework, developed by the National Institute of Standards and Technology (NIST).

NIST Cybersecurity Framework provides a comprehensive set of guidelines and best practices for organizations to manage and reduce cybersecurity risk.

Another well-known framework is the ISO 27001, which is part of the ISO/IEC 27000 series.

ISO 27001 is an international standard that outlines the requirements for establishing, implementing, maintaining, and continually improving an information security management system (ISMS).

To comply with ISO 27001, organizations must assess their information security risks, implement controls and safeguards, and regularly monitor and evaluate their security posture.

The Payment Card Industry Data Security Standard (PCI DSS) is another important compliance standard, primarily applicable to organizations that handle payment card data.

PCI DSS sets requirements for securing payment card data, including encryption, access control, and regular security assessments.

Organizations that process payment card transactions must adhere to PCI DSS to protect sensitive financial information.

The Health Insurance Portability and Accountability Act (HIPAA) is a compliance standard specifically designed for healthcare organizations.

HIPAA mandates stringent security and privacy measures to safeguard protected health information (PHI).

Organizations in the healthcare industry must comply with HIPAA to ensure the confidentiality, integrity, and availability of PHI.

In addition to these specific frameworks and standards, various industry-specific regulations and legal requirements may apply to organizations.

For instance, the General Data Protection Regulation (GDPR) in Europe sets strict rules for the protection of personal data.

Organizations that handle personal data of European Union citizens must comply with GDPR, which includes requirements related to data protection, privacy, and breach notification.

To ensure compliance with these frameworks and standards, organizations must adopt a systematic approach to assess their current security posture and identify gaps or areas of non-compliance.

This typically involves conducting a security risk assessment to identify vulnerabilities and threats, as well as assessing the effectiveness of existing security controls.

One of the essential aspects of compliance is documentation. Organizations must maintain records of their security policies, procedures, and control implementations to demonstrate compliance during audits or assessments.

This documentation serves as evidence that the organization is following established guidelines and standards.

Additionally, organizations may need to conduct periodic security audits and assessments to evaluate their ongoing compliance with the selected frameworks and standards.

These assessments may involve internal reviews or external audits conducted by independent third-party assessors.

Organizations can utilize various tools and technologies to help them achieve and maintain compliance.

For instance, vulnerability scanning tools can identify security weaknesses that need to be addressed to align with specific standards.

Encryption technologies can be deployed to protect sensitive data, as required by many compliance standards.

Security information and event management (SIEM) solutions can help organizations monitor their network and systems for security incidents, which is a fundamental requirement for compliance.

Moreover, organizations can implement access control mechanisms and authentication procedures to ensure that only authorized personnel have access to sensitive systems and data.

To facilitate compliance efforts, many organizations use Governance, Risk, and Compliance (GRC) software solutions that streamline the management of compliance requirements, risk assessments, and audit activities.

These tools can help organizations track their progress toward compliance, manage documentation, and generate reports for auditing purposes.

It's important to note that compliance is an ongoing process, and organizations must continuously assess and update their security measures to adapt to evolving threats and changes in regulations.

This includes staying informed about updates and revisions to compliance frameworks and standards, as they can impact an organization's compliance efforts.

To demonstrate compliance during audits or assessments, organizations should prepare by ensuring that their documentation is up-to-date, conducting regular security assessments, and addressing any identified vulnerabilities or gaps promptly.

Overall, compliance frameworks and standards play a pivotal role in enhancing an organization's security posture and ensuring that they meet industry-specific requirements and legal obligations.

By adhering to these guidelines and best practices, organizations can not only protect their data and systems but also build trust with their customers, partners, and stakeholders by demonstrating a commitment to cybersecurity and data privacy.

Risk assessment and mitigation strategies are essential components of any robust cybersecurity program, helping organizations identify, analyze, and manage potential threats and vulnerabilities.

Effective risk assessment enables organizations to proactively identify and prioritize risks to their information assets and infrastructure.

One common approach to risk assessment is the use of risk matrices, which provide a visual representation of the likelihood and impact of specific risks.

To conduct a risk assessment, organizations should begin by identifying all potential threats and vulnerabilities that could affect their systems, data, or operations.

This includes both internal and external threats, such as malware, insider threats, natural disasters, and cyberattacks.

Once potential risks are identified, organizations should evaluate the likelihood of each risk occurring and the potential impact it could have on the organization's operations.

This assessment should consider factors such as the organization's industry, geographic location, and the value of the assets at risk.

To assess likelihood and impact, organizations can use qualitative or quantitative methods.

Qualitative methods involve using expert judgment to assign subjective values to likelihood and impact, often on a scale of low, medium, or high.

Quantitative methods involve using historical data and mathematical models to estimate the probability and financial impact of specific risks.

After assessing risks, organizations should prioritize them based on their likelihood and potential impact.

This prioritization helps organizations focus their resources and efforts on addressing the most critical risks first.

To prioritize risks, organizations can use risk matrices, risk scoring models, or other risk assessment tools.

Once risks are prioritized, organizations can develop mitigation strategies to reduce the likelihood and impact of these risks.

Mitigation strategies should be tailored to the specific risks identified and may include a combination of technical, administrative, and physical controls.

For example, to mitigate the risk of a data breach, an organization may implement encryption, access controls, and employee training programs.

To mitigate the risk of a natural disaster, an organization may implement backup and disaster recovery solutions and relocate critical systems to a secure data center.

To deploy these mitigation strategies, organizations should create a detailed risk mitigation plan that outlines the specific controls and actions to be taken to address each risk.

This plan should include responsible parties, timelines, and success criteria.

Once the risk mitigation plan is developed, organizations should implement the identified controls and monitor their effectiveness regularly.

This may involve conducting vulnerability assessments, penetration testing, and security audits to identify weaknesses and ensure that controls are functioning as intended.

In addition to implementing controls, organizations should also establish incident response and business continuity plans to address potential security incidents and disruptions to operations.

These plans outline the steps to be taken in the event of a security incident or disaster and help organizations minimize the impact on their operations and recover quickly.

To deploy an incident response plan, organizations should define incident categories and severity levels, establish an incident response team, and create communication and notification procedures.

They should also conduct regular incident response drills and exercises to ensure that personnel are prepared to respond effectively to incidents.

Similarly, business continuity plans should outline the critical systems and processes that need to be maintained during a disruption and specify recovery time objectives (RTOs) and recovery point objectives (RPOs).

To deploy a business continuity plan, organizations should identify alternative locations, resources, and personnel to ensure that critical operations can continue in the event of a disruption.

Regular testing and updating of these plans are essential to ensure their effectiveness. In addition to proactive risk assessment and mitigation, organizations should also have a robust monitoring and detection capability to identify and respond to emerging threats.

This includes the use of intrusion detection systems (IDS), intrusion prevention systems (IPS), and security information and event management (SIEM) solutions to monitor network traffic and system logs for signs of suspicious activity.

To deploy these monitoring and detection capabilities, organizations should configure these tools to generate alerts and notifications when anomalies or potential security threats are detected.

Furthermore, organizations should establish an incident response team and incident response procedures to investigate and respond to security incidents promptly.

To facilitate risk assessment and mitigation efforts, organizations should regularly review and update their risk assessment, mitigation plans, and incident response and business continuity plans.

This should be done in response to changes in the threat landscape, organizational structure, or technology environment.

It's also important for organizations to stay informed about emerging threats and vulnerabilities through threat intelligence feeds, security advisories, and industry publications.

In summary, risk assessment and mitigation strategies are fundamental to effective cybersecurity.

By identifying, analyzing, and prioritizing risks and implementing appropriate controls and plans, organizations can strengthen their security posture and reduce their exposure to potential threats and vulnerabilities.

Furthermore, ongoing monitoring and incident response capabilities are crucial for detecting and responding to emerging threats and incidents effectively.

By adopting a proactive approach to risk assessment and mitigation, organizations can better protect their information assets and ensure the resilience of their operations in the face of evolving cybersecurity challenges.

Chapter 9: Business Continuity and Disaster Recovery

Business Impact Analysis (BIA) is a critical process within the field of business continuity and disaster recovery planning.

It is aimed at identifying and assessing the potential impact of various disruptions and disasters on an organization's operations and processes.

BIA provides organizations with valuable insights into the dependencies and criticality of different functions, helping them prioritize recovery efforts and allocate resources effectively.

The primary objective of conducting a BIA is to determine how long an organization can afford to be without specific functions or systems before experiencing significant financial losses or operational setbacks.

To initiate a BIA, organizations should first establish a cross-functional team that includes representatives from various departments and business units.

This team should be led by a business continuity manager or coordinator who has experience in conducting BIAs and understands the organization's objectives and operations.

The first step in the BIA process is to identify all critical business processes and functions.

These are the activities and systems that are essential for the organization to achieve its strategic goals and fulfill its obligations to stakeholders.

Critical functions can vary from one organization to another, depending on its industry, size, and specific business objectives.

Once the critical functions are identified, the next step is to determine the maximum allowable downtime (MAD) for each of them.

MAD represents the maximum amount of time a function can be disrupted before it starts causing significant harm to the organization.

For example, a financial institution may have a very low MAD for its online banking system due to customer expectations for 24/7 access.

On the other hand, a non-profit organization may have a higher MAD for its donor management system.

After determining MAD, the BIA team should assess the potential financial and operational impacts of disruptions to each critical function.

This assessment should consider factors such as lost revenue, increased operating costs, reputational damage, legal and regulatory compliance, and customer and stakeholder expectations.

Quantifying these impacts can be challenging, but it is essential to have a realistic estimate of the potential consequences of a disruption.

The BIA team should work closely with financial and operational stakeholders to gather the necessary data and input for this assessment.

Once the impact assessment is complete, the BIA team can use the information to prioritize critical functions based on their MAD and potential impact.

Functions with a low MAD and high potential impact should be considered top priorities for recovery efforts.

Conversely, functions with a high MAD and lower potential impact may not require immediate attention during a disruptive event.

At this stage, the BIA team should also identify and document the dependencies between critical functions.

These dependencies can include technology systems, data, personnel, and external partners or suppliers.

Understanding these dependencies is crucial because a disruption to one function may have a cascading effect on others.

For instance, if a data center hosting critical systems fails, it can impact multiple functions that rely on those systems.

To document dependencies, the BIA team can use tools like flowcharts, diagrams, or narrative descriptions.

Additionally, the team should identify and assess any mitigation strategies or controls in place for each critical function.

These controls can include redundancy in technology systems, backup data centers, or business continuity plans.

The BIA team should evaluate the effectiveness of these controls in reducing the risk of disruptions and minimizing their potential impact.

If controls are insufficient or require improvement, the team should make recommendations for enhancing them.

After completing the BIA process, organizations should compile the findings into a comprehensive report that outlines the critical functions, MAD, impact assessments, dependencies, and recommended mitigation strategies.

This report serves as a valuable resource for business continuity and disaster recovery planning.

It helps organizations prioritize their recovery efforts, allocate resources effectively, and develop actionable plans for maintaining or restoring critical functions during disruptive events.

Furthermore, the BIA report can be used to justify investments in risk mitigation and business continuity initiatives to senior management and stakeholders.

One of the essential aspects of a BIA is its role in shaping an organization's business continuity and disaster recovery plans.

The information gathered through the BIA process informs the development of specific strategies and tactics for ensuring the continuity of critical functions in the event of disruptions.

For example, based on the BIA findings, an organization may decide to invest in redundant technology systems or establish offsite data backups to reduce downtime during an IT system failure.

The BIA also guides the development of recovery time objectives (RTOs) and recovery point objectives (RPOs) for critical functions.

RTO represents the targeted time for restoring a function to full operation, while RPO represents the maximum allowable data loss during a disruption.

These objectives are crucial for designing recovery plans and allocating resources appropriately.

To deploy the findings of a BIA effectively, organizations should integrate them into their broader business continuity and disaster recovery planning processes.

This includes creating detailed recovery plans for each critical function, specifying roles and responsibilities for recovery teams, and conducting regular testing and exercises to ensure that recovery plans are effective.

Regular updates to the BIA are also essential to account for changes in the organization's operations, technology landscape, or risk profile.

In summary, Business Impact Analysis is a vital process that helps organizations understand the criticality of their functions, assess the potential impact of disruptions, and prioritize recovery efforts.

By conducting a BIA and incorporating its findings into business continuity and disaster recovery planning, organizations can enhance their resilience and minimize the impact of disruptive events.

Effective BIA processes provide the foundation for informed decision-making, resource allocation, and risk mitigation strategies, ultimately contributing to an organization's ability to withstand and recover from disruptions successfully.

Disaster recovery planning and testing are crucial components of an organization's overall business continuity strategy.

Disasters, whether natural or man-made, can have severe consequences for businesses, including data loss, downtime, and financial losses.

Disaster recovery planning involves creating a comprehensive strategy for how an organization will respond to and recover from disasters.

This strategy encompasses all aspects of an organization's operations, including IT systems, data, personnel, and facilities.

One fundamental aspect of disaster recovery planning is the development of a disaster recovery plan (DRP).

A DRP is a documented set of procedures and guidelines that outline the steps to be taken in the event of a disaster.

It includes details on how to assess the extent of the damage, prioritize recovery efforts, and implement recovery procedures.

A well-crafted DRP should also specify roles and responsibilities for personnel involved in the recovery process.

To initiate the disaster recovery planning process, organizations should establish a cross-functional team that includes representatives from IT, operations, security, and other relevant departments.

This team should be responsible for developing, implementing, and maintaining the DRP.

The first step in creating a DRP is to identify potential disaster scenarios that could impact the organization.

These scenarios can vary widely, from natural disasters like earthquakes and floods to man-made events like cyberattacks and data breaches.

To ensure that all relevant scenarios are considered, organizations should conduct a thorough risk assessment as part of their disaster recovery planning process.

A risk assessment helps organizations identify vulnerabilities and assess the likelihood and potential impact of various disaster scenarios.

For example, in the case of a data center hosting critical systems, a risk assessment may consider the likelihood of a power outage, equipment failure, or a security breach and the potential impact on operations.

Once potential disaster scenarios are identified, organizations can prioritize them based on their likelihood and potential impact.

This prioritization helps organizations allocate resources and focus their efforts on the most critical scenarios.

For example, a financial institution may prioritize scenarios that could result in financial losses, such as a cyberattack or a disruption to payment processing systems.

To deploy a disaster recovery plan effectively, organizations should establish recovery time objectives (RTOs) and recovery point objectives (RPOs) for each critical system and function.

RTO represents the targeted time for restoring a system or function to full operation, while RPO represents the maximum allowable data loss during a disruption.

These objectives help organizations set clear expectations for recovery efforts and guide the development of recovery strategies.

For example, for a critical customer-facing website, the RTO may be set at four hours, meaning that the organization aims to have the website fully operational within four hours of a disruption.

Similarly, the RPO may be set at 15 minutes, indicating that the organization can tolerate a maximum of 15 minutes of data loss.

To achieve these objectives, organizations must implement appropriate recovery strategies and solutions.

These strategies can include data backups, failover systems, redundant data centers, and cloud-based disaster recovery services.

For example, to meet a short RTO for a critical database, organizations may replicate data in real-time to a secondary data center.

This ensures that the database can be quickly switched over to the secondary data center in the event of a disruption.

Regular testing and exercises are essential aspects of disaster recovery planning.

Testing helps organizations ensure that their recovery strategies and procedures work as intended and that personnel are prepared to respond effectively to disasters.

One common testing method is the disaster recovery tabletop exercise.

In a tabletop exercise, the disaster recovery team gathers to simulate a disaster scenario and walk through the steps of the recovery plan.

This exercise helps identify any gaps or weaknesses in the plan and allows for adjustments and improvements.

To deploy a tabletop exercise, organizations can follow these steps:

Define the scenario: Choose a realistic disaster scenario that aligns with the organization's risk profile and objectives. For example, simulate a cyberattack that disrupts IT systems.

Assemble the team: Invite key stakeholders and members of the disaster recovery team to participate in the exercise. This may include IT personnel, business continuity managers, and external partners if applicable.

Walk through the scenario: Present the chosen scenario to the participants and guide them through the steps of the recovery plan. Encourage open discussion and problem-solving.

Identify strengths and weaknesses: During the exercise, document both the strengths and weaknesses of the recovery plan and procedures. This feedback will be valuable for making improvements.

Review and update the plan: Based on the feedback and insights gained from the tabletop exercise, review and update the disaster recovery plan as needed. Ensure that any identified weaknesses are addressed.

Repeat regularly: Conduct tabletop exercises on a regular basis, at least annually, to keep the disaster recovery team and stakeholders engaged and prepared.

Another crucial aspect of disaster recovery planning is data backup and recovery.

Data is often one of an organization's most valuable assets, and losing it can have severe consequences.

To protect against data loss, organizations should implement robust backup and recovery strategies.

One common approach is the use of regular data backups.

Organizations should schedule regular backups of critical data, applications, and systems to ensure that up-to-date copies are available in the event of a data loss incident.

To deploy data backups effectively, organizations can follow these steps:

Identify critical data: Determine which data is critical to the organization's operations and should be included in the backup plan.

Define backup frequency: Establish a backup schedule that includes the frequency of backups, such as daily, weekly, or monthly, based on the criticality of the data.

Select backup methods: Choose backup methods and technologies that align with the organization's needs, such as full backups, incremental backups, or continuous data replication.

Choose backup locations: Determine where backup copies will be stored. This can include on-premises backup servers, offsite data centers, or cloud-based storage solutions.

Test data recovery: Regularly test the data recovery process to ensure that backups can be successfully restored when needed. Maintain backup documentation: Keep thorough documentation of backup schedules, procedures, and contact information for personnel responsible for data recovery.

Monitor backup status: Implement monitoring and alerting mechanisms to track the status of backups and ensure they are completed successfully.

In addition to data backups, organizations should also consider business continuity planning and disaster recovery testing.

Business continuity planning focuses on ensuring that essential business functions can continue during and after a disaster.

It includes strategies for maintaining operations, communication, and customer service, even in challenging circumstances.

To deploy an effective business continuity plan, organizations can follow these steps:

Identify critical business functions: Determine which business functions are essential for the organization's survival and prioritize them accordingly.

Develop business continuity strategies: Create strategies and tactics for maintaining critical functions during a disaster, such as relocating employees to a backup facility or enabling remote work.

Establish communication plans: Develop communication plans for informing employees, customers, and stakeholders about the organization's response to a disaster.

Train personnel: Ensure that employees are trained and prepared to execute their roles in the business continuity plan.

Conduct regular drills: Practice the business continuity plan through drills and exercises to identify any issues or areas for improvement.

Review and update the plan: Continuously review and update the business continuity plan to reflect changes in the organization's operations, technology, and risk landscape.

Coordinate with disaster recovery: Ensure that the business continuity plan aligns with the disaster recovery plan, and both plans work seamlessly together.

Disaster recovery testing is the process of validating and evaluating the effectiveness of disaster recovery plans and procedures.

Testing helps organizations identify weaknesses in their plans and provides an opportunity to make necessary adjustments.

To deploy disaster recovery testing effectively, organizations can follow these steps:

Define testing objectives: Clearly define the objectives and scope of the disaster recovery test. Determine what aspects of the plan will be tested, such as data recovery, system failover, or personnel response.

Plan the test scenario: Design a realistic test scenario that simulates a disaster or disruptive event. Consider various scenarios, such as a data center outage, a cybersecurity breach, or a natural disaster.

Assemble a testing team: Form a testing team that includes members of the disaster recovery and business continuity teams, IT personnel, and relevant stakeholders.

Execute the test: Implement the test scenario and follow the disaster recovery plan's procedures. Document the test's progress, including any issues or challenges encountered.

Evaluate the results: Assess the test's results against predefined objectives. Identify any areas of improvement or gaps in the plan.

Make necessary adjustments: Based on the test results, make adjustments to the disaster recovery plan and procedures to address any weaknesses or deficiencies.

Document and report: Document the test results, lessons learned, and any changes made to the plan. Share the findings with relevant stakeholders and leadership.

Repeat regularly: Conduct disaster recovery testing on a regular basis, at least annually, to ensure that the plan remains effective and up-to-date.

In summary, disaster recovery planning and testing are critical components of an organization's resilience against disruptions.

By developing comprehensive disaster recovery plans, setting clear objectives, and regularly testing and refining recovery procedures, organizations can minimize the impact of disasters and ensure continuity of operations.

Effective disaster recovery planning encompasses risk assessment, data backup strategies, business continuity planning, and thorough testing, all of which contribute to an organization's ability to recover swiftly and efficiently from disasters of various scales and types.

Chapter 10: Cyber Resilience Implementation and Future Trends

Implementing cyber resilience within an organization is a complex and multi-faceted process that requires careful planning, dedicated resources, and a clear roadmap.

This roadmap outlines the key steps and considerations for effectively implementing cyber resilience measures to enhance an organization's ability to withstand and recover from cyber threats.

Assessment and Gap Analysis: The journey towards cyber resilience begins with a comprehensive assessment of an organization's current cybersecurity posture.

CLI Command: **nmap -sV -O target_ip** (To perform a basic network scan and gather information about open ports and services running on the target system).

During this phase, organizations can utilize tools like vulnerability scanners, penetration testing, and security audits to identify weaknesses and vulnerabilities.

The assessment should also take into account regulatory requirements, industry standards, and best practices.

Establishing a Cyber Resilience Team: To drive the implementation of cyber resilience, it's essential to establish a dedicated team responsible for planning, executing, and monitoring resilience measures.

CLI Command: **useradd -m -d /home/cyber_resilience_team cyber_resilience_user** (To create a new user account for a member of the cyber resilience team).

The team should include cybersecurity experts, incident responders, business continuity professionals, and executives who can provide leadership and support.

Defining Cyber Resilience Objectives: Organizations should clearly define their objectives for cyber resilience.

These objectives should align with the organization's overall business goals and risk tolerance.

CLI Command: **echo "Our cyber resilience objective is to ensure uninterrupted business operations while effectively responding to and recovering from cyber incidents." >> resilience_objectives.txt** (To document and communicate the resilience objectives).

Defining specific, measurable, and achievable goals is essential for tracking progress.

Developing a Cyber Resilience Strategy: Based on the assessment and objectives, organizations should develop a comprehensive cyber resilience strategy.

This strategy should include plans for incident response, disaster recovery, business continuity, and crisis management.

CLI Command: **touch cyber_resilience_strategy.doc** (To create a document for outlining the cyber resilience strategy).

It should also encompass measures for threat detection, threat prevention, and threat mitigation.

Investing in Cybersecurity Technologies: To implement effective cyber resilience, organizations must invest in appropriate cybersecurity technologies.

CLI Command: **apt-get install snort** (To install the Snort intrusion detection system, a common cybersecurity technology).

This includes firewalls, intrusion detection systems, antivirus software, encryption tools, and advanced threat detection solutions.

The choice of technologies should align with the organization's risk assessment and strategy.

Employee Training and Awareness: Human error is a common factor in cybersecurity incidents.

Organizations should invest in cybersecurity training and awareness programs for employees at all levels.

Explanation: Training programs can include simulated phishing exercises, security awareness workshops, and ongoing education about the latest threats and best practices.

Ensuring that employees are aware of their role in cyber resilience is crucial.

Incident Response Plan: Organizations should develop a well-documented incident response plan (IRP) that outlines procedures for identifying, containing, and mitigating cyber incidents.

Explanation: The IRP should include clear roles and responsibilities for the cyber resilience team, communication protocols, and predefined steps for notifying stakeholders and law enforcement if necessary.

Regular tabletop exercises should be conducted to test the effectiveness of the IRP.

Data Protection and Backup: Ensuring the confidentiality and availability of critical data is paramount for cyber resilience.

CLI Command: **rsync -avz /important_data/ backup_server:/backup_location/** (To perform a data backup using rsync).

Organizations should implement data encryption, access controls, and regular data backups to protect against data loss.

Backup strategies should be tested and verified to ensure data can be restored in case of an incident.

Continuous Monitoring and Threat Intelligence: Establishing continuous monitoring of network traffic and system activity is essential for early threat detection.

CLI Command: **tcpdump -i eth0 -n -v -s0 -w capture.pcap** (To capture network traffic for analysis using the tcpdump tool).

Threat intelligence feeds and security information and event management (SIEM) systems can provide valuable insights into emerging threats.

Organizations should proactively gather and analyze threat intelligence to adapt their cyber resilience strategies.

Third-Party Risk Management: Many organizations rely on third-party vendors and partners.

CLI Command: **nmap -p 80,443 target_vendor_domain** (To scan a vendor's website for open ports).

Implementing a third-party risk management program helps ensure that vendors adhere to cybersecurity standards and do not introduce vulnerabilities into the organization's ecosystem.

Regular Testing and Validation: Cyber resilience measures should be regularly tested and validated through simulations and exercises.

CLI Command: **nikto -h target_url** (To scan a web application for known vulnerabilities using the Nikto scanner).

Organizations can conduct red team exercises, penetration tests, and disaster recovery drills to evaluate their readiness.

Incident Reporting and Learning: Encouraging a culture of incident reporting and learning from incidents is vital for continuous improvement.

Explanation: Organizations should have a process in place for reporting and analyzing incidents, whether they are successful cyberattacks or near misses.

Lessons learned should be integrated into the cyber resilience strategy to strengthen defenses.

Regulatory Compliance: Depending on the industry, organizations may need to comply with various cybersecurity regulations and standards.

CLI Command: **auditd** (To enable the Linux audit framework for monitoring and compliance purposes).

Compliance with these requirements should be part of the cyber resilience strategy and regularly assessed.

Communication and Public Relations: In the event of a significant cyber incident, effective communication with stakeholders, the media, and the public is crucial.

Explanation: Organizations should have a communication plan in place that includes designated spokespersons, key messages, and a coordinated response.

Transparent and timely communication can help maintain trust and minimize reputational damage.

Continuous Improvement: Cyber resilience is an ongoing process.

CLI Command: **git commit -m "Cyber resilience strategy update"** (To commit changes to the cyber resilience strategy documentation).

Organizations should regularly review and update their cyber resilience strategy, taking into account emerging threats, technology advancements, and lessons learned from incidents and exercises.

In summary, implementing cyber resilience is a strategic imperative for organizations in an increasingly digital and interconnected world.

By following this roadmap and addressing these key areas, organizations can enhance their ability to withstand and recover from cyber threats while minimizing the impact on their operations, reputation, and customers.

In the ever-evolving landscape of cybersecurity, staying ahead of emerging trends is essential for organizations seeking to enhance their cyber resilience.

One of the prominent trends in cyber resilience is the increasing sophistication of cyber threats, driven by advancements in technology and techniques used by threat actors.

To address this, organizations are adopting more proactive and intelligence-driven approaches to threat detection and response.

For instance, Security Information and Event Management (SIEM) systems, coupled with Artificial Intelligence (AI) and Machine Learning (ML), are becoming crucial tools for identifying anomalies and potential threats within vast datasets.

These technologies can analyze large volumes of data in real-time, helping organizations detect and respond to threats faster and more accurately.

Another emerging trend is the integration of cyber resilience with broader business resilience strategies.

This holistic approach recognizes that cyber threats are just one component of the overall risk landscape that organizations face.

By aligning cyber resilience with business continuity and disaster recovery efforts, organizations can ensure a more comprehensive and coordinated response to disruptions of all kinds, whether they are cyber-related or not.

The Internet of Things (IoT) presents a growing challenge and opportunity for cyber resilience.

The proliferation of IoT devices in homes and businesses introduces new attack vectors and vulnerabilities.

Organizations are investing in IoT security solutions and developing strategies to protect both their own IoT devices and those of their customers and partners.

This includes measures such as securing device firmware, encrypting data transmitted by IoT devices, and monitoring for suspicious behavior.

Cloud adoption continues to grow, and with it comes the need for robust cloud security and resilience strategies.

As organizations migrate their data and operations to the cloud, they must ensure that their chosen cloud providers have strong security measures in place.

Additionally, organizations must implement cloud-specific security controls and practices to protect their assets and data in the cloud environment.

With the rise of remote work and the proliferation of mobile devices, endpoint security has become a critical focus for organizations.

Mobile devices are often the first point of entry for cyberattacks, and securing them is paramount.

This includes implementing mobile device management (MDM) solutions, enforcing strong authentication methods, and regularly updating and patching mobile operating systems and applications.

Supply chain attacks have gained prominence in recent years as a method for threat actors to infiltrate organizations indirectly.

These attacks target vulnerabilities in an organization's supply chain, compromising the security of products and services delivered to them.

Organizations are now taking a more proactive approach to assess and secure their supply chains, including conducting thorough security assessments of third-party vendors.

The use of multi-factor authentication (MFA) is becoming increasingly standard practice for enhancing access control and authentication.

MFA requires users to provide two or more forms of authentication before granting access, adding an extra layer of security.

Many organizations are implementing MFA not only for remote access but also for internal systems and applications.

As the threat landscape evolves, organizations are recognizing the importance of threat intelligence sharing and collaboration.

Information sharing allows organizations to stay informed about emerging threats and vulnerabilities and to respond more effectively.

This trend has led to the formation of industry-specific Information Sharing and Analysis Centers (ISACs) and increased participation in government-sponsored information sharing programs.

The adoption of DevSecOps practices is also on the rise, integrating security into the software development and deployment process from the outset.

This proactive approach ensures that security is not an afterthought but an integral part of the development lifecycle.

DevSecOps involves automated security testing, continuous monitoring, and collaboration between development, security, and operations teams.

The use of Artificial Intelligence (AI) and Machine Learning (ML) for cybersecurity purposes is gaining momentum.

These technologies can analyze vast amounts of data to identify patterns and anomalies that may be indicative of cyber threats.

They can also automate response actions, such as isolating compromised devices or blocking malicious traffic.

However, the use of AI and ML in cybersecurity also presents challenges, such as the potential for false positives and the need for robust data privacy measures.

Blockchain technology, known for its use in cryptocurrencies like Bitcoin, is also finding applications in cybersecurity.

Blockchain can enhance the security and integrity of data by providing a tamper-proof and transparent ledger of transactions and activities.

Organizations are exploring the use of blockchain for secure authentication, identity management, and data protection.

The convergence of Operational Technology (OT) and Information Technology (IT) networks is creating new cyber resilience challenges for critical infrastructure organizations.

As OT systems become more connected to IT networks, they are exposed to the same cyber threats.

Organizations in critical sectors such as energy, transportation, and healthcare are investing in robust cybersecurity measures to protect their OT environments.

Ransomware attacks continue to be a significant threat, with threat actors becoming more aggressive and demanding larger ransoms.

Organizations are focusing on improving their backup and recovery capabilities, implementing security awareness training, and enhancing email security to combat ransomware.

As technology evolves, so do the methods and tactics of cybercriminals.

Organizations must remain vigilant, adapt to emerging trends, and continuously improve their cyber resilience strategies to stay one step ahead of evolving cyber threats.

By embracing these trends and proactively addressing emerging challenges, organizations can enhance their cyber resilience and better protect their assets, data, and reputation in an increasingly interconnected and digital world.

BOOK 4
TROJAN EXPOSED
RED TEAM TACTICS AND ETHICAL HACKING

ROB BOTWRIGHT

Chapter 1: The Art of Ethical Hacking

Ethical hacking methodologies are essential tools for organizations seeking to identify and address vulnerabilities in their systems and networks.

These methodologies provide a systematic and structured approach to ethical hacking, enabling security professionals to conduct authorized penetration testing and security assessments.

One widely adopted ethical hacking methodology is the Open Web Application Security Project (OWASP) Testing Guide.

The OWASP Testing Guide is a comprehensive resource that covers various aspects of web application security testing.

It includes detailed testing checklists and guidance on how to test for common vulnerabilities such as SQL injection, cross-site scripting (XSS), and insecure session management.

Another popular ethical hacking methodology is the Penetration Testing Execution Standard (PTES).

PTES provides a standardized framework for conducting penetration tests, emphasizing the importance of thorough reconnaissance, vulnerability analysis, and exploitation.

The methodology also emphasizes post-exploitation activities, such as privilege escalation and data exfiltration, to simulate real-world attack scenarios.

The Information Systems Security Assessment Framework (ISSAF) is another ethical hacking methodology designed to assist security professionals in assessing the security of information systems.

ISSAF covers a wide range of assessment techniques, including network mapping, vulnerability scanning, and password cracking.

It also provides guidance on conducting physical security assessments and social engineering attacks.

When conducting ethical hacking assessments, it's essential to follow a structured methodology to ensure thorough coverage and effective results.

One commonly used methodology for network penetration testing is the Certified Information Systems Security Professional (CISSP) methodology.

This methodology involves a series of steps, including information gathering, vulnerability analysis, and exploitation.

During the information gathering phase, ethical hackers use various tools and techniques to gather information about the target network, such as scanning for open ports and identifying active services.

Once the initial reconnaissance is complete, the ethical hacker proceeds to the vulnerability analysis phase.

In this phase, the hacker identifies potential vulnerabilities in the target network, including misconfigurations, outdated software, and weak passwords.

Vulnerability scanning tools, such as Nessus and OpenVAS, can be used to automate this process.

After identifying vulnerabilities, the ethical hacker proceeds to the exploitation phase, where they attempt to exploit the identified weaknesses to gain unauthorized access to the target network.

This may involve executing exploits, brute-forcing passwords, or leveraging social engineering techniques.

Throughout the ethical hacking assessment, it's crucial to maintain a detailed log of all actions taken, as well as any findings or discoveries.

This log serves as a record of the assessment and helps in documenting the vulnerabilities and their associated risks.

In addition to following a structured methodology, ethical hackers must also adhere to a strict code of ethics and obtain proper authorization before conducting assessments.

Ethical hacking should always be performed with the full knowledge and consent of the organization being tested.

Unauthorized hacking is illegal and unethical and can result in legal consequences.

When conducting ethical hacking assessments, it's essential to use the right tools and techniques for the job.

There is a wide range of cybersecurity tools available to ethical hackers, each designed to address specific tasks and objectives.

For example, tools like Nmap and Wireshark are commonly used for network reconnaissance and traffic analysis.

Burp Suite is a popular tool for web application testing, while Metasploit provides a comprehensive framework for penetration testing and exploitation.

When using these tools, ethical hackers must ensure that they are using them responsibly and in compliance with legal and ethical standards.

In addition to using tools, ethical hackers often need to write and execute custom scripts and code to automate specific tasks or exploits.

Scripting languages like Python and PowerShell are commonly used for this purpose, as they provide the flexibility and power required for ethical hacking tasks.

Ethical hackers should also be proficient in using the command-line interface (CLI) of various operating systems, as it allows for more fine-grained control and customization of hacking tools and techniques.

To gain authorized access to systems and networks during ethical hacking assessments, ethical hackers may require valid credentials or tokens.

In some cases, they may need to use password cracking tools or techniques to obtain access.

One common approach is to use a brute-force attack, where the hacker attempts to guess the password by trying different combinations of characters systematically.

Tools like Hydra and John the Ripper are commonly used for password cracking tasks.

Social engineering is another critical aspect of ethical hacking, as it involves manipulating individuals into divulging confidential information or performing actions that compromise security.

Ethical hackers may use social engineering techniques, such as phishing emails or pretexting, to trick employees into providing sensitive information or clicking on malicious links.

To defend against social engineering attacks, organizations should provide security awareness training to their employees and implement strict access controls.

Overall, ethical hacking methodologies are a vital component of cybersecurity, helping organizations identify and address vulnerabilities before malicious hackers can exploit them.

By following structured methodologies, using the right tools and techniques, and obtaining proper authorization, ethical hackers play a crucial role in strengthening cybersecurity defenses and protecting sensitive information.

In the realm of cybersecurity and ethical hacking, understanding the legal and ethical considerations is paramount.

Conducting ethical hacking assessments must always be carried out within the boundaries of the law.

Unauthorized hacking is illegal and can lead to severe consequences, including criminal charges and civil lawsuits.

To ensure compliance with the law, ethical hackers must obtain explicit authorization from the organization or individual responsible for the systems being tested.

This authorization is typically documented in a legally binding agreement, commonly known as a "penetration testing agreement" or "ethical hacking agreement."

The agreement outlines the scope, objectives, and limitations of the ethical hacking assessment, as well as the terms and conditions governing the engagement.

It is essential for ethical hackers to review and understand the terms of the agreement thoroughly before proceeding with any testing.

Once the authorization is granted, ethical hackers must limit their activities to the scope defined in the agreement.

Deviation from the agreed-upon scope can result in legal and ethical complications.

For example, if the ethical hacker strays beyond the authorized systems or conducts activities not explicitly permitted, they may be subject to legal action.

It's also essential to respect the privacy and confidentiality of sensitive information discovered during an ethical hacking assessment.

Ethical hackers may encounter sensitive data, such as personally identifiable information (PII) or proprietary business information.

Handling this data with the utmost care and ensuring it is not disclosed or misused is both a legal and ethical responsibility.

Encryption and secure data handling practices should be employed to protect any data obtained during testing.

During ethical hacking assessments, ethical hackers often interact with target systems, networks, and applications.

This interaction must be conducted in a manner that minimizes disruption and inconvenience to the organization.

In cases where testing may affect system availability or performance, the organization should be notified in advance and agree to the potential impact.

Furthermore, ethical hackers should avoid causing any damage or data loss during their assessments.

If unintentional damage occurs, it should be reported immediately to the organization for resolution.

When conducting ethical hacking assessments, it is essential to adhere to a strict code of ethics.

The most widely recognized code of ethics for ethical hackers is provided by the International Council of Electronic Commerce

Consultants (EC-Council) and is known as the "Certified Ethical Hacker (CEH) Code of Ethics."

This code emphasizes principles such as honesty, integrity, and professionalism.

Ethical hackers must act with integrity, maintain confidentiality, and avoid conflicts of interest.

They should also continually strive to improve their skills and stay up-to-date with the latest security trends and techniques.

Furthermore, ethical hackers should report any vulnerabilities and findings to the organization promptly.

This enables the organization to take necessary steps to remediate the issues and enhance its security posture.

Failure to report vulnerabilities or exploiting them for personal gain is considered unethical and can lead to legal consequences.

Ethical hackers must also be aware of potential legal liabilities associated with their activities.

Even with proper authorization, ethical hacking assessments can sometimes trigger alarm systems or be misconstrued as malicious activity.

It is advisable for ethical hackers to have legal counsel or legal advisors available to provide guidance in case of legal challenges.

Organizations should also maintain records of the ethical hacking engagement, including the authorization documentation, test results, and any communication related to the assessment.

These records can serve as evidence of compliance with legal and ethical standards.

In some jurisdictions, there may be specific laws and regulations governing cybersecurity and ethical hacking activities.

Ethical hackers should be familiar with the legal landscape in their region and ensure their activities are compliant.

Furthermore, ethical hackers should be cautious when conducting assessments across international boundaries, as legal requirements may vary significantly.

Some countries have stringent regulations related to cybersecurity and data privacy, and activities that are legal in one jurisdiction may be prohibited in another.

To ensure compliance with international laws, ethical hackers should seek legal advice and guidance when conducting assessments that involve cross-border activities.

In summary, ethical hacking is a valuable tool for identifying and addressing security vulnerabilities, but it must be conducted with strict adherence to legal and ethical considerations.

Obtaining explicit authorization, respecting privacy and confidentiality, and following a code of ethics are essential aspects of ethical hacking.

Being aware of potential legal liabilities and seeking legal guidance when necessary is crucial to conducting ethical hacking assessments responsibly and effectively.

Chapter 2: Understanding Red Team Operations

In the world of cybersecurity, the concept of Red Team vs. Blue Team dynamics plays a pivotal role in strengthening an organization's security posture.

These two teams, often referred to as the Red Team and the Blue Team, work together to assess and improve an organization's security defenses.

The Red Team represents the offensive side of cybersecurity, simulating the actions of malicious hackers attempting to breach an organization's systems.

Their primary goal is to identify vulnerabilities and weaknesses within the organization's infrastructure and applications.

The Blue Team, on the other hand, represents the defensive side, responsible for safeguarding the organization's assets and data against cyber threats.

They are tasked with monitoring and defending the organization's systems, responding to security incidents, and implementing security measures to mitigate risks.

The concept of Red Team vs. Blue Team dynamics is often used in a practice known as "Red Team vs. Blue Team exercises" or "adversarial testing."

These exercises involve the Red Team launching simulated attacks on the organization's systems, while the Blue Team defends against these attacks in a controlled and monitored environment.

One of the primary goals of Red Team vs. Blue Team exercises is to uncover vulnerabilities and weaknesses that may not be apparent through traditional security assessments.

The Red Team uses a variety of tactics, techniques, and procedures (TTPs) to emulate real-world threats.

These may include spear-phishing attacks, network reconnaissance, exploitation of known vulnerabilities, and social engineering.

The Red Team may also employ custom-developed exploits and malware to test the organization's defenses thoroughly.

In contrast, the Blue Team's role is to detect and respond to the Red Team's actions effectively.

They leverage various security tools and technologies, such as intrusion detection systems (IDS), intrusion prevention systems (IPS), security information and event management (SIEM) systems, and endpoint detection and response (EDR) solutions.

The Blue Team continuously monitors network traffic, logs, and system activity to identify suspicious or malicious behavior.

When they detect a potential threat or security incident, they respond by investigating the incident, mitigating the threat, and taking actions to prevent further damage.

One of the key benefits of Red Team vs. Blue Team exercises is that they provide organizations with a more holistic view of their security posture.

Traditional security assessments, such as vulnerability scanning or penetration testing, may uncover known vulnerabilities but may not capture the full spectrum of risks.

Red Team vs. Blue Team exercises allow organizations to assess their readiness to defend against sophisticated and evolving threats.

These exercises also help organizations improve their incident response capabilities by providing practical experience in handling security incidents.

In a Red Team vs. Blue Team exercise, both teams collaborate to create realistic attack scenarios and objectives.

The Red Team sets specific goals and objectives, such as gaining unauthorized access to critical systems, exfiltrating sensitive data, or disrupting business operations.

The Blue Team, meanwhile, establishes a defense strategy to protect the organization's assets and data.

They develop incident response procedures, identify critical assets, and implement security controls to detect and respond to potential threats.

Throughout the exercise, the Red Team and Blue Team engage in a constant cycle of attack and defense.

The Red Team attempts to achieve their objectives while the Blue Team works to detect, respond to, and mitigate the Red Team's actions.

The exercise may include a series of attack phases, with the Red Team adjusting their tactics based on the Blue Team's defensive measures.

The outcome of a Red Team vs. Blue Team exercise is not solely focused on success or failure.

Instead, it is an opportunity for both teams to learn and improve.

After the exercise concludes, a detailed debriefing session takes place, where both teams share their experiences and insights.

This feedback loop helps organizations identify areas for improvement in their security defenses and incident response procedures.

Red Team vs. Blue Team dynamics also promote a collaborative and proactive security culture within an organization.

By simulating real-world threats and testing their defenses, organizations can enhance their cybersecurity resilience and readiness.

Ultimately, the goal is to strengthen the organization's security posture and reduce the risk of successful cyberattacks.

In summary, Red Team vs. Blue Team dynamics are a critical component of modern cybersecurity practices.

These exercises provide organizations with valuable insights into their security vulnerabilities and incident response capabilities.

By working together, the Red Team and Blue Team help organizations identify weaknesses, improve their defenses, and enhance their overall cybersecurity resilience.

The practice of red teaming is a proactive approach to cybersecurity that revolves around specific goals and objectives.

At its core, red teaming seeks to simulate real-world cyber threats and attacks, providing organizations with a comprehensive assessment of their security posture.

The primary goal of red teaming is to identify vulnerabilities, weaknesses, and gaps in an organization's defenses that might otherwise go unnoticed.

Through simulated attacks and adversary emulation, red teaming helps organizations discover hidden risks and potential points of entry for cyber adversaries.

A crucial objective of red teaming is to assess an organization's ability to detect and respond to security incidents effectively.

By challenging the organization's incident response capabilities, red teaming ensures that any breaches or security breaches can be detected promptly and mitigated.

Red teaming also aims to evaluate the organization's cybersecurity policies, procedures, and adherence to security best practices.

This includes assessing whether security controls, such as firewalls, intrusion detection systems, and access controls, are correctly configured and functioning as intended.

Another key objective of red teaming is to provide actionable recommendations for improving an organization's security posture.

The insights gained from red teaming exercises can help organizations prioritize security investments and make informed decisions about risk mitigation strategies.

Furthermore, red teaming fosters a proactive security mindset within the organization, encouraging continuous improvement and a commitment to security excellence.

To achieve these goals and objectives, red teaming involves several critical activities and methodologies.

One fundamental aspect of red teaming is reconnaissance, where the red team gathers information about the target organization, its systems, and its employees.

This information is crucial for planning realistic attack scenarios and crafting effective social engineering tactics.

Social engineering, such as phishing attacks, is a common technique used by red teams to assess an organization's susceptibility to manipulation and deception.

These attacks aim to trick employees into revealing sensitive information or performing actions that could compromise security.

In addition to social engineering, red teams employ a variety of technical attacks to assess an organization's vulnerability to exploitation.

This may include attempting to exploit known vulnerabilities in software, applications, or operating systems.

For example, a red team may use a vulnerability scanner to identify weaknesses in the organization's infrastructure and then attempt to exploit those vulnerabilities to gain unauthorized access.

Once access is achieved, the red team simulates lateral movement within the network, attempting to escalate privileges and access sensitive data or systems.

Throughout these activities, the red team documents their findings, including the vulnerabilities exploited, the methods used, and the effectiveness of the organization's security controls.

This documentation is essential for providing a detailed assessment of the organization's security posture.

At the conclusion of a red teaming exercise, the red team and the organization's security team engage in a thorough debriefing and analysis.

This phase allows both teams to discuss the findings, assess the impact of simulated attacks, and develop recommendations for improving security.

The red team provides insights into the techniques and tactics used during the exercise, highlighting areas where the organization's defenses were successful and where they may need improvement.

The organization's security team, in turn, shares their experiences and observations, helping to identify opportunities for enhancing security policies and procedures.

One critical outcome of red teaming is the generation of a comprehensive report that details the findings, recommendations, and lessons learned from the exercise.

This report serves as a valuable resource for the organization's leadership and decision-makers, guiding their efforts to enhance cybersecurity.

In summary, the goals and objectives of red teaming are centered around identifying vulnerabilities, evaluating incident response capabilities, assessing security policies and procedures, and providing actionable recommendations for improving cybersecurity.

Through simulated attacks and adversary emulation, red teaming helps organizations strengthen their security posture and foster a proactive security mindset.

Chapter 3: Reconnaissance and Information Gathering

Passive reconnaissance techniques are a fundamental aspect of information gathering in cybersecurity.

They involve collecting data and information about a target, such as an organization, system, or individual, without directly interacting with the target or raising any suspicions.

Passive reconnaissance serves as the initial phase of the reconnaissance process, where cybersecurity professionals or threat actors gather intelligence to plan further actions.

One of the primary objectives of passive reconnaissance is to identify potential weaknesses and vulnerabilities that can be exploited in later stages of an attack.

One common passive reconnaissance technique is open-source intelligence (OSINT) gathering.

OSINT involves collecting publicly available information from various sources, such as websites, social media, forums, and news articles.

Cybersecurity professionals use OSINT to gather information about an organization's online presence, including its website structure, domain names, email addresses, and employee information.

Threat actors, on the other hand, may use OSINT to identify potential targets or vulnerabilities for malicious purposes.

To perform passive reconnaissance effectively, cybersecurity professionals and threat actors use a combination of tools and techniques.

One widely used technique is DNS enumeration, which involves querying the domain name system (DNS) to gather information about domain names, subdomains, and their associated IP addresses.

This technique can help identify the organization's online infrastructure and web applications.

For example, a cybersecurity professional can use the "nslookup" command to query a domain's DNS records and retrieve valuable information.

The command may look like this:

Copy code

```
nslookup example.com
```

The results will include the domain's IP address and possibly other subdomains or mail servers associated with the domain.

Another passive reconnaissance technique involves email harvesting.

Email addresses are valuable pieces of information that can be leveraged for phishing attacks, social engineering, or other malicious purposes.

Tools like "theHarvester" can automate the process of collecting email addresses associated with a domain.

The command to use "theHarvester" may look like this:

cssCopy code

```
theHarvester -d example .com -l 100 - b google
```

This command instructs the tool to search Google for email addresses related to the domain "example.com" and limits the results to 100.

Passive reconnaissance also includes footprinting, which focuses on gathering information about the target's network infrastructure.

Cybersecurity professionals use network scanning tools like "Nmap" to discover open ports, services, and potential vulnerabilities on a target's network.

The following command scans a target IP address for open ports:

cssCopy code

```
nmap -p 1-65535 target_IP
```

This command scans all 65,535 possible ports on the target IP address.

Similarly, threat actors may use the same techniques to identify exposed services and potential entry points.

In passive reconnaissance, information is often gathered about an organization's employees, including their names, job titles, and roles.

This information can be valuable for crafting targeted spear-phishing attacks or social engineering attempts.

Cybersecurity professionals and threat actors may leverage LinkedIn and other social media platforms to collect such data.

Automated tools like "LinkedIn-Scraper" can facilitate this process.

Passive reconnaissance can also involve searching for publicly available documents and files that may reveal sensitive information.

For example, searching for file extensions like .pdf, .doc, or .xls on a target's website may yield documents containing valuable data.

The "site:" operator in search engines can be used to narrow down search results to a specific domain.

For instance:

makefileCopy code

site:example.com filetype:pdf

This query searches for PDF files specifically on the "example.com" domain.

In summary, passive reconnaissance techniques are a crucial component of cybersecurity and threat intelligence.

They involve gathering information about a target organization or individual without direct interaction or raising suspicions.

These techniques rely on tools and methods such as DNS enumeration, email harvesting, footprinting, and searching for publicly available documents.

Both cybersecurity professionals and threat actors employ passive reconnaissance, albeit with different intentions and ethical considerations.

Active reconnaissance, also known as active scanning or probing, is a critical phase in the reconnaissance process that follows passive reconnaissance and involves more direct interaction with the target.

Unlike passive reconnaissance, active reconnaissance techniques require an entity, whether it's a cybersecurity professional or a threat actor, to engage with the target's systems or network actively.

Active reconnaissance serves several purposes, including identifying live systems, open ports, and potential vulnerabilities.

One of the primary tools used for active reconnaissance is the popular network scanning tool called "Nmap."

To scan a target's network actively, you can use the following command:

cssCopy code

```
nmap -T4 -A -v target_IP
```

In this command:

-T4 sets the timing template to aggressive, which increases the scan speed.

-A enables OS detection, version detection, script scanning, and traceroute.

-v increases the verbosity of the output, providing more detailed information.

When conducting active reconnaissance, it's crucial to be aware that such actions can trigger alerts and alarms in the target's intrusion detection system (IDS) or firewall logs.

Therefore, it's essential to proceed with caution and, if necessary, obtain proper authorization or permissions to conduct active scanning on a network.

Active reconnaissance also includes footprinting, which involves gathering information about a target's network infrastructure, systems, and services.

This information helps in creating a comprehensive map of the target's attack surface and potential entry points for exploitation.

Footprinting may involve techniques such as DNS querying, network mapping, and service identification.

Another important aspect of active reconnaissance is port scanning.

Port scanning is the process of sending requests to a target's system to identify open ports, services running on those ports, and potentially vulnerable services.

Nmap is a versatile tool for conducting port scans. You can specify the range of ports to scan using the **-p** option. For example:

cssCopy code

```
nmap -p 1-100 target_IP
```

This command scans ports 1 through 100 on the target's IP address.

While conducting active reconnaissance, it's crucial to maintain a low profile and avoid actions that could disrupt the target's network or services.

Intrusive scans, such as those that send a large volume of traffic, can attract unwanted attention and potentially lead to countermeasures being deployed by the target.

It's also essential to perform active reconnaissance with a specific goal in mind, such as identifying vulnerabilities or weaknesses that can be exploited.

For example, if a cybersecurity professional is conducting an authorized penetration test, the objective may be to discover potential security flaws that need to be addressed.

However, if a threat actor is performing active reconnaissance, the goal may be to identify weaknesses that can be exploited for malicious purposes.

In both cases, proper documentation of findings and adherence to ethical guidelines are essential.

Active reconnaissance techniques also include network scanning to identify live hosts and systems within a target's network.

One common technique is the "ping sweep," which sends ICMP echo requests to a range of IP addresses to determine which hosts are online.

The "ping" command can be used for this purpose. For example:

rCopy code

```
ping -c 3 target_IP_range
```

This command sends three ICMP echo requests to a range of IP addresses, and if a response is received, it indicates that the host is online.

In summary, active reconnaissance is a critical phase in the reconnaissance process that involves direct interaction with the target's systems and network.

Tools like Nmap are commonly used for active reconnaissance, including port scanning, network mapping, and service identification.

Proper authorization, discretion, and ethical considerations are essential when conducting active reconnaissance, whether for security testing or malicious purposes.

Chapter 4: Vulnerability Assessment and Exploitation

Vulnerability scanning and assessment are crucial components of cybersecurity that help organizations identify and mitigate potential security weaknesses in their systems and networks.

These processes involve systematically searching for vulnerabilities, assessing their severity, and taking appropriate measures to address them.

One widely used tool for vulnerability scanning is OpenVAS (Open Vulnerability Assessment System).

To initiate a vulnerability scan with OpenVAS, you can use the following command:

sqlCopy code

openvas -start

This command starts the OpenVAS scanner and begins the scanning process.

Vulnerability scanning aims to identify known vulnerabilities in software, hardware, and configurations.

It typically involves scanning network devices, servers, web applications, and other assets to detect weaknesses that could be exploited by attackers.

Once vulnerabilities are identified, they are often categorized based on their severity and potential impact on the organization.

Common vulnerability databases, such as the National Vulnerability Database (NVD) and the Common Vulnerability and Exposure (CVE) system, provide information about known vulnerabilities and their associated risk levels.

Organizations use the results of vulnerability scans to prioritize and address vulnerabilities based on their criticality.

To further assess the impact and potential exploitation of vulnerabilities, penetration testing or ethical hacking may be conducted.

Penetration testing involves simulating real-world attacks to determine if vulnerabilities can be exploited to gain unauthorized access or compromise systems.

One tool commonly used for penetration testing is Metasploit, which provides a framework for developing and executing exploit code.

To run a Metasploit scan, you can use the following command:
Copy code

```
msfconsole
```

This command opens the Metasploit Framework console, where you can access various modules and exploit options.

During vulnerability assessment and penetration testing, it's essential to follow a structured approach to ensure thorough coverage.

One widely adopted framework is the Open Web Application Security Project (OWASP) Top Ten, which lists the most critical web application security risks.

The OWASP Top Ten includes vulnerabilities such as injection attacks, broken authentication, and security misconfigurations.

Another critical aspect of vulnerability assessment is vulnerability management.

Vulnerability management involves the process of identifying, prioritizing, and remediating vulnerabilities in a systematic manner.

This process often includes:

Vulnerability Identification: Identifying vulnerabilities through scanning and assessment.

Risk Assessment: Evaluating the potential impact and likelihood of exploitation for each vulnerability.

Prioritization: Ranking vulnerabilities based on risk factors, including severity, business impact, and exploitability.

Remediation Planning: Developing a plan to address vulnerabilities, which may involve patching, configuration changes, or other security measures.

Remediation Execution: Implementing the remediation plan to mitigate or eliminate vulnerabilities.

Verification: Confirming that vulnerabilities have been successfully remediated through re-scanning or testing.

Reporting: Documenting the entire vulnerability management process, including findings, actions taken, and compliance with security policies.

Vulnerability scanning and assessment tools are continuously updated to keep pace with evolving threats and vulnerabilities.

Many organizations also use automated patch management systems to streamline the deployment of security updates and patches to address known vulnerabilities.

Additionally, vulnerability scanners often offer features for compliance monitoring, allowing organizations to ensure that their systems and configurations adhere to industry standards and security best practices.

In summary, vulnerability scanning and assessment are integral parts of a comprehensive cybersecurity strategy.

These processes help organizations proactively identify and address security weaknesses in their systems and networks, reducing the risk of security breaches and data compromises.

Exploiting vulnerabilities safely is a critical aspect of ethical hacking and penetration testing, as it allows security professionals to assess the security posture of systems and applications without causing harm.

The primary goal of safe exploitation is to identify weaknesses and vulnerabilities in a controlled environment, without negatively impacting the target system or network.

To achieve safe exploitation, it is crucial to follow a structured and ethical approach that prioritizes the security of the target and adheres to legal and ethical guidelines.

One common approach to safe exploitation is to conduct penetration testing in a controlled and isolated testing environment, often referred to as a "sandbox" or "testbed."

A sandbox is a secure and isolated environment where security professionals can simulate attacks, exploit vulnerabilities, and assess the security of systems without affecting the production environment.

Using a sandbox allows testers to safely explore and exploit vulnerabilities without risking data loss, service disruption, or legal consequences.

To create a sandbox environment, security professionals can set up a virtualized or isolated network segment using virtualization technology or network segmentation techniques.

Virtualization platforms like VMware, VirtualBox, or Hyper-V enable testers to create virtual machines (VMs) that mimic real-world systems.

For example, to create a virtual Windows machine for testing, one can use the following steps:

Install a virtualization platform like VirtualBox.

Create a new virtual machine, specifying the desired operating system (e.g., Windows) and configuration settings.

Install the operating system and necessary software on the virtual machine.

Set up network isolation to prevent the virtual machine from accessing the production network.

Once the sandbox environment is set up, testers can safely deploy vulnerable applications, services, or systems within the isolated network segment.

To simulate attacks and exploit vulnerabilities safely, security professionals can use tools and techniques commonly employed in penetration testing.

For example, penetration testers often use Metasploit, a penetration testing framework that provides a wide range of exploit modules and payloads.

To launch Metasploit and select an exploit module, one can use the following command:

Copy code

```
msfconsole
```

This opens the Metasploit Framework console, where testers can search for exploit modules and customize payloads to simulate attacks safely.

It's essential to emphasize that ethical hackers and penetration testers must obtain proper authorization and consent before conducting any exploitation activities.

Unauthorized or malicious exploitation can lead to legal consequences and damage to systems and data.

To ensure ethical and safe exploitation, security professionals should follow a well-defined penetration testing methodology, such as the Penetration Testing Execution Standard (PTES) or the Open Web Application Security Project (OWASP) Testing Guide.

These methodologies provide guidelines for conducting penetration tests, including steps for vulnerability discovery, exploitation, and reporting.

During the exploitation phase, testers aim to demonstrate the impact of vulnerabilities by gaining unauthorized access, escalating privileges, or executing malicious code.

Testers must document their actions carefully, including the specific steps taken, the vulnerabilities exploited, and the potential impact on the target system.

Once the penetration test is complete, testers should provide a comprehensive report to the organization or client, detailing the findings, including vulnerabilities discovered and recommended remediation steps.

In summary, exploiting vulnerabilities safely is a fundamental aspect of ethical hacking and penetration testing, allowing security professionals to assess the security of systems and applications without causing harm.

By following ethical guidelines, using controlled environments, and obtaining proper authorization, testers can identify weaknesses, assess risk, and help organizations improve their security posture.

Chapter 5: Penetration Testing Methodologies

Penetration testing, often referred to as pen testing, is a structured and systematic approach to evaluating the security of computer systems, networks, and applications.

It involves simulating real-world attacks to identify vulnerabilities and weaknesses that could be exploited by malicious actors.

Penetration testing is a critical component of a comprehensive cybersecurity strategy, helping organizations proactively assess their security posture and mitigate potential risks.

The process of penetration testing typically consists of several distinct phases, each with its own objectives and activities.

Preparation Phase:

The first phase involves planning and preparation.

The penetration testing team defines the scope of the test, including the target systems, applications, and network segments to be assessed.

Goals and objectives are established to align with the organization's specific security needs.

Authorization and consent are obtained from the organization or client to conduct the test.

Reconnaissance Phase:

In this phase, the testers gather information about the target environment.

They collect data such as IP addresses, domain names, email addresses, and employee information.

Open-source intelligence (OSINT) techniques, online research, and tools like "whois" and "nslookup" may be used to gather information.

Scanning Phase:

Testers conduct active scanning to identify live hosts, open ports, and services running on the target systems.

Tools like Nmap or Nessus are commonly used for network and vulnerability scanning.

The goal is to discover potential entry points and vulnerabilities that can be exploited.

Enumeration Phase:

During enumeration, testers gather additional information about the target systems and services.

They may perform banner grabbing to identify specific software versions, enumerate users, and identify potential vulnerabilities.

Enumeration helps testers narrow down potential attack vectors.

Vulnerability Analysis Phase:

Testers analyze the results of scanning and enumeration to identify vulnerabilities.

Vulnerabilities can range from misconfigurations and outdated software to known security weaknesses.

The goal is to prioritize vulnerabilities based on their severity and potential impact.

Exploitation Phase:

In this phase, testers attempt to exploit the identified vulnerabilities to gain unauthorized access or control over target systems.

Exploitation may involve using known exploits or developing custom exploits.

The goal is to demonstrate the impact of the vulnerabilities and assess their real-world risk.

Post-Exploitation Phase:

After gaining access, testers may escalate privileges, maintain persistence, and explore the target environment.

They aim to determine the extent of potential damage that could be caused by an attacker with unauthorized access.

Post-exploitation activities are conducted with caution and ethical considerations.

Reporting Phase:

The final phase involves documenting the results of the penetration test.

Testers prepare a comprehensive report that includes findings, vulnerabilities, exploitation details, and recommended remediation steps.

The report helps the organization understand its security weaknesses and prioritize mitigation efforts.

Cleanup and Remediation:

Testers ensure that any changes made during the test are reverted, and systems are returned to their original state.

The organization can then begin addressing the identified vulnerabilities and implementing security measures.

Post-Testing Review:

After the penetration test, a post-testing review may be conducted to assess the effectiveness of the test and gather feedback.

Lessons learned can help improve future testing processes and overall security.

Penetration testing is an ongoing process that should be conducted regularly to adapt to changing threats and technologies.

It is a valuable tool for organizations seeking to proactively identify and address security weaknesses, ultimately enhancing their cybersecurity posture and reducing the risk of security breaches.

Penetration testing relies heavily on a wide range of tools and techniques that are essential for identifying vulnerabilities and assessing the security of target systems, networks, and applications.

One of the fundamental tools used in penetration testing is the command-line interface (CLI), which allows testers to interact directly with a system or network. For instance, they can use the "ping" command to determine if a target host is reachable and responsive.

Beyond basic CLI commands, penetration testers often use specialized tools and techniques to automate tasks and conduct comprehensive assessments.

One such tool is "Nmap" (Network Mapper), a powerful open-source network scanning tool that can discover hosts, open ports, and services running on a network. To scan a target network, testers can use the following CLI command:

Copy code

```
nmap -v -sV target_ip
```

The "-v" flag enables verbose output, and the "-sV" flag performs service version detection on open ports.

Another commonly used tool is "Metasploit," a penetration testing framework that offers a vast collection of exploits, payloads, and auxiliary modules. Testers can use Metasploit to simulate attacks and exploit vulnerabilities. To start Metasploit, they can enter:

Copy code

```
msfconsole
```

This opens the Metasploit Framework console, where testers can search for exploits and interact with modules.

For web application testing, "Burp Suite" is a popular choice. It's an integrated platform for web security testing, including scanning for vulnerabilities like SQL injection and Cross-Site Scripting (XSS). Testers can use Burp Suite to capture and analyze HTTP traffic.

To analyze network traffic and packets, testers may employ "Wireshark." This open-source packet analyzer allows for real-time inspection of network protocols. They can start Wireshark with:

Copy code

```
wireshark
```

Wireless network assessments often require the use of "Aircrack-ng," a suite of tools for auditing wireless networks. It can be used to capture, crack, and analyze Wi-Fi traffic. For instance, to crack a WEP-encrypted Wi-Fi network, testers can use:

cssCopy code

```
aircrack-ng          -a1        -b       00:11:22:33:44:55
captured_packet_file.cap
```

Penetration testers also utilize scripting languages like Python and Ruby to develop custom scripts and tools for their assessments. These languages offer flexibility and the ability to create tailored exploits and automation.

For information gathering and OSINT (Open-Source Intelligence), testers can use tools like "theHarvester," which collects email addresses, subdomains, and other data from various sources. To run theHarvester, they can execute:

cssCopy code

```
theHarvester -d target_domain -b google
```

Additionally, "DirBuster" and "Gobuster" are useful for brute-forcing directories and files on web servers to discover hidden content.

In terms of exploitation, testers may employ "Hydra" for password cracking attacks, "Sqlmap" for automated SQL injection tests, and "Nikto" for scanning web servers for vulnerabilities.

To conduct wireless assessments, "Reaver" and "Bully" are tools for cracking WPS-enabled Wi-Fi networks. For wireless packet injection and analysis, "Packet Injection Test" tools such as "aireplay-ng" are essential.

Social engineering assessments often involve sending phishing emails. Testers can use "PhishingFrenzy" or "GoPhish" to create and send simulated phishing campaigns to test an organization's susceptibility to such attacks.

For privilege escalation and post-exploitation, "PowerShell Empire" and "Mimikatz" are commonly used tools on Windows systems.

It's important to note that while these tools can be powerful for penetration testing, they should only be used in authorized and ethical assessments with proper consent from the organization or system owner. Unauthorized use of such tools can have legal consequences.

Furthermore, penetration testers must constantly update and expand their toolkits to adapt to evolving threats and technologies, ensuring that they have the right tools for the job and can effectively identify vulnerabilities to improve an organization's security posture.

Chapter 6: Advanced Social Engineering Techniques

Psychological manipulation plays a crucial role in the realm of social engineering, serving as a potent tool in the hands of malicious actors seeking to exploit human vulnerabilities.

Social engineering is a tactic that relies on manipulating individuals into divulging confidential information, granting unauthorized access, or performing actions against their own best interests.

One of the key psychological principles underpinning social engineering is the human tendency to trust others, often without question. Malicious actors leverage this trust to establish rapport and credibility, creating a false sense of security.

One common technique used in social engineering is "pretexting," where an attacker fabricates a plausible scenario or pretext to elicit sensitive information. For instance, an attacker might impersonate a technical support agent and call a target, claiming to need their login credentials for system maintenance.

Another psychological manipulation tactic is "phishing," which involves sending deceptive emails or messages that appear to be from legitimate sources. Phishing emails often contain urgent or enticing content, such as fake security alerts, to trick recipients into clicking malicious links or providing personal information.

"Authority" is a powerful psychological trigger exploited by social engineers. People tend to comply with requests from perceived authority figures. Attackers may impersonate high-ranking executives or law enforcement officers to manipulate targets into complying with their demands.

The "scarcity" principle leverages the fear of missing out. Attackers might claim that a limited-time offer or opportunity is available, pressuring individuals to take immediate action without considering the risks.

Social engineers also employ "liking" tactics, attempting to build rapport with their targets by finding common interests, expressing sympathy, or feigning friendliness. These tactics make it easier to manipulate individuals into providing information or taking actions they otherwise wouldn't.

The "consistency and commitment" principle is utilized to exploit a person's desire to maintain consistency in their actions and beliefs. Attackers may start with small, harmless requests and gradually escalate to more significant demands, as individuals are more likely to comply when they've already agreed to a series of requests.

Additionally, the "reciprocity" principle exploits the human inclination to reciprocate favors. Social engineers may offer assistance or seemingly helpful information to create a sense of obligation in their targets, leading them to provide information or access in return.

"Social proof" relies on the tendency to follow the crowd. Attackers may create a sense of urgency or social pressure by falsely claiming that others have already taken a certain action, convincing targets to do the same.

"Scarcity" and "urgency" are commonly used in phishing attacks. Attackers might claim that a target's account will be locked unless they click on a provided link and provide their login credentials immediately.

The "fear" principle leverages people's instinctive responses to threats. Attackers may send intimidating messages, such as fake legal notices or threats of account suspension, to manipulate individuals into complying with their demands out of fear.

To illustrate these psychological manipulation tactics in action, consider a scenario where an attacker impersonates an IT technician and calls an employee, claiming there's been a security breach. They use the "authority" principle by stating that they are from the IT department and assert that immediate action is required to prevent further damage.

The attacker employs the "urgency" principle by insisting that the employee must follow their instructions without delay. They create a sense of fear by emphasizing the potential consequences of not complying, such as data loss or financial penalties.

Using the "liking" principle, the attacker attempts to establish rapport by expressing understanding of the employee's concerns and promising to resolve the issue swiftly. They also utilize "social proof" by mentioning that several colleagues have already followed their instructions, implying that compliance is the norm.

In this scenario, the attacker successfully manipulates the employee's psychology, leading them to disclose sensitive information and grant unauthorized access. Understanding these psychological manipulation tactics is crucial for individuals and organizations to recognize and defend against social engineering attacks effectively.

Phishing attacks are a prevalent and insidious form of cyber threat that aim to deceive individuals into divulging sensitive information or performing actions that benefit malicious actors.

These attacks typically involve the use of deceptive emails, messages, or websites that mimic legitimate sources, luring victims into believing they are interacting with a trustworthy entity.

One of the primary objectives of phishing attacks is to steal personal information, such as login credentials, credit card numbers, or social security numbers, which can be exploited for financial gain or identity theft.

Phishing attacks often start with a seemingly innocent email that appears to be from a reputable organization or contact. Attackers may impersonate banks, e-commerce platforms, social media networks, or even government agencies to gain the trust of recipients.

These phishing emails frequently contain urgent or alarming messages, creating a sense of urgency and panic. For example, a phishing email might claim that the recipient's bank account has been compromised and that immediate action is required to prevent unauthorized transactions.

To enhance the illusion of legitimacy, attackers may employ various techniques, such as using company logos, mimicking email addresses, and replicating the layout of legitimate websites.

One of the critical components of a phishing attack is the malicious link or attachment embedded within the email. Clicking on the link can lead the victim to a fake website that prompts them to enter sensitive information, which is then captured by the attackers.

In some cases, the attachment itself contains malware that, when opened, can infect the victim's device and grant attackers unauthorized access.

Spear phishing is a more targeted and sophisticated variant of phishing. In spear phishing attacks, attackers research their victims extensively to craft personalized and convincing messages.

The goal of spear phishing is often to compromise specific individuals or organizations rather than casting a wide net. Attackers may gather information about a target's interests, job role, colleagues, or recent events to tailor their emails accordingly.

For example, an attacker targeting a corporate executive might send an email that appears to be from a colleague or business partner, discussing a recent industry conference they both attended. This personalized approach increases the chances of the victim falling for the scam.

Spear phishing attacks have been responsible for numerous high-profile breaches and data leaks. Attackers may use the information gathered through spear phishing to gain unauthorized access to sensitive systems, steal intellectual property, or launch further attacks from within the victim's network.

To mitigate the risks of falling victim to phishing and spear phishing attacks, individuals and organizations must adopt several security best practices.

One essential precaution is to verify the authenticity of emails, especially those requesting sensitive information or urgent actions. Recipients should check email addresses, hover over links to preview the actual URL, and contact the sender directly using trusted contact information to confirm the request.

Another critical measure is to enable multi-factor authentication (MFA) wherever possible, which adds an extra layer of security by requiring users to provide a second form of verification, such as a one-time code sent to their mobile device.

Educating employees and individuals about the dangers of phishing is equally crucial. Training programs can help individuals recognize the signs of phishing attacks and teach them how to respond appropriately.

Organizations can also implement email filtering and anti-phishing solutions to detect and block malicious emails before they reach employees' inboxes. Additionally, regular software updates and patches should be applied to protect against known vulnerabilities that attackers might exploit.

Phishing and spear phishing attacks are constantly evolving, with attackers employing increasingly sophisticated tactics to deceive their targets. Therefore, ongoing vigilance and proactive cybersecurity measures are essential to combat these threats effectively.

Chapter 7: Privilege Escalation and Post-Exploitation

Elevating privileges on compromised systems is a crucial step for attackers seeking to gain greater control and access within a target network.

Once an attacker has successfully infiltrated a system, they often begin with limited permissions, typically running with the rights and privileges of the user or application they initially compromised.

However, to carry out more extensive and damaging actions, such as installing malware, exfiltrating sensitive data, or compromising critical network infrastructure, attackers need elevated privileges that provide them with more control over the compromised system.

Elevating privileges involves obtaining higher-level access rights, such as those of an administrator or root user, which grants the attacker broader authority to execute commands, manipulate system configurations, and access sensitive resources.

Attackers employ various techniques to elevate privileges on compromised systems, and these methods can vary depending on the operating system, system architecture, and security measures in place.

One common method for elevating privileges is exploiting vulnerabilities in the system's software or configuration. This may involve exploiting a software vulnerability, such as a buffer overflow, that allows the attacker to execute arbitrary code with higher-level privileges.

To exploit vulnerabilities, attackers may use command-line tools or scripts designed to target specific weaknesses in the system. For instance, they might use a tool like "Metasploit" to search for known vulnerabilities and launch attacks against them. An example of a Metasploit command to exploit a vulnerability could be:

perlCopy code

```
use exploit/windows/local/ms17_010_psexec
```

This Metasploit module targets the MS17-010 vulnerability to execute code as SYSTEM on a compromised Windows system, effectively elevating privileges.

Another technique for privilege escalation involves taking advantage of misconfigurations or weak security settings within the system. Attackers may search for improperly configured permissions or weak passwords to escalate their privileges.

To manipulate permissions, attackers may use command-line utilities available on the compromised system. For example, on a Unix-based system, they might use the "chmod" command to change file permissions, or on a Windows system, they might use the "icacls" command to modify access control lists (ACLs).

An example of changing file permissions using the "chmod" command on a Unix-based system:

bashCopy code

```
chmod +s /bin/bash
```

This command sets the setuid bit on the "/bin/bash" binary, allowing any user who runs it to gain the privileges of the file's owner.

In cases where attackers have obtained valid login credentials, they may leverage those credentials to access higher-level accounts with elevated privileges. This often involves using techniques like password cracking or password guessing to compromise administrator or root accounts.

Command-line tools like "Hydra" or "John the Ripper" can be employed for brute-force attacks to crack passwords. For instance, the following is an example of using Hydra to perform a brute-force attack on an SSH server:

arduinoCopy code

```
hydra -l username -P passwordlist.txt ssh://targethost
```

Attackers can also exploit weaknesses in the system's configuration to gain elevated privileges. This might involve manipulating environment variables, modifying system files, or exploiting weak security policies.

For example, an attacker might modify the "sudoers" file on a Unix-based system to grant themselves elevated privileges without needing to enter a password.

bashCopy code

```
echo "attacker ALL=(ALL:ALL) NOPASSWD: ALL" >> /etc/sudoers
```

This command appends a line to the "sudoers" file, allowing the user "attacker" to execute commands as any user without a password prompt.

Privilege escalation is a critical concern for both attackers and defenders in the realm of cybersecurity. Attackers seek to gain more control and access, while defenders aim to prevent, detect, and mitigate these actions.

Organizations can defend against privilege escalation by implementing strong access controls, regularly patching and updating software, monitoring for unusual activities, and enforcing the principle of least privilege, ensuring that users and processes only have the minimum necessary permissions to perform their tasks.

In summary, elevating privileges on compromised systems is a pivotal step for attackers, enabling them to expand their influence and carry out more damaging actions. Understanding these techniques is essential for both cybersecurity professionals defending against attacks and those studying cybersecurity to gain insights into the tactics used by malicious actors.

Maintaining persistence and lateral movement are advanced techniques employed by cyber adversaries to extend their presence within a compromised network and continue their malicious activities over an extended period.

Once an attacker has successfully gained initial access to a network or system, their next objective is often to ensure that they can maintain access even if their initial point of entry is discovered and closed by network defenders.

One common method for maintaining persistence involves creating backdoors or persistent implants that allow the attacker to regain access even if their initial entry point is detected and removed.

To create a backdoor, an attacker may use command-line tools or custom malware to establish a hidden, persistent connection to the compromised system. This can be done using a variety of techniques, including adding malicious registry entries on Windows systems or configuring cron jobs on Unix-based systems.

For example, an attacker might use the "at" command on a Windows system to schedule a task that runs a malicious script: rCopy code

```
at          01:00          /every:M,T,W,Th,F,S,Su
C:\path\to\malicious_script.bat
```

This command schedules the execution of the malicious script every day at 01:00, ensuring persistent access to the compromised system.

In some cases, attackers may deploy rootkits or kernel-level malware that modify the operating system to maintain persistence. Rootkits can be extremely stealthy, making them difficult to detect.

For lateral movement within a network, attackers use various techniques to move from one compromised system to another, gradually expanding their control and access. This allows them to explore the network, steal data, and compromise additional systems.

Common lateral movement techniques involve abusing legitimate network protocols and services to move laterally. For example, an attacker might use the Windows Management

Instrumentation Command-line (WMIC) tool to execute commands on remote systems:

sqlCopy code

```
wmic /node:remotecomputer process call create "cmd.exe /c malicious_command"
```

This command allows the attacker to execute malicious commands on the remote computer using legitimate administrative tools.

Another technique is to abuse Remote Desktop Protocol (RDP) or SSH to connect to remote systems. If an attacker has valid credentials or has compromised an account with access, they can use these protocols to move laterally.

To use RDP, an attacker might use the "mstsc" command on a Windows system:

bashCopy code

```
mstsc /v:remotecomputer /admin
```

This command opens a remote desktop session to the target system, allowing the attacker to interact with it.

Similarly, for SSH on Unix-based systems:

cssCopy code

```
ssh username @remotecomputer
```

Once inside a remote system, attackers can explore and compromise additional systems within the network, often escalating privileges as they go.

Additionally, attackers may use exploitation techniques to move laterally, searching for vulnerabilities in unpatched systems or misconfigured services. They may use command-line tools or custom scripts to exploit these weaknesses and gain access to other systems.

For example, an attacker might use the "EternalBlue" exploit to target a vulnerable Windows system and gain unauthorized access:

Copy code

```
ms17-010-exploit.py
```

This Python script exploits the MS17-010 vulnerability to compromise a remote Windows system, demonstrating how attackers can exploit vulnerabilities for lateral movement.

Defending against these advanced techniques requires a multi-faceted approach. Organizations should implement robust security measures, such as intrusion detection systems (IDS), intrusion prevention systems (IPS), and endpoint detection and response (EDR) solutions to detect and respond to unusual activities and known attack patterns.

Regularly patching and updating systems and software is crucial to eliminate known vulnerabilities. Additionally, implementing strong access controls, segmenting the network, and employing least privilege principles can limit an attacker's ability to move laterally.

Security professionals must stay informed about emerging threats and tactics used by cyber adversaries to continuously adapt and improve their defense strategies. Understanding these techniques is essential for defenders to stay one step ahead of attackers and protect their networks and systems effectively.

Chapter 8: Evading Detection and Covering Tracks

Anti-forensics and data destruction techniques are employed by individuals or entities seeking to conceal their digital activities and erase traces of their presence in computer systems or networks.

These techniques pose a significant challenge to digital forensic investigators who rely on the integrity and availability of digital evidence to solve crimes, gather intelligence, or assess security incidents.

Anti-forensics encompasses a wide range of methods designed to undermine or disrupt the forensic examination process. One common anti-forensic technique involves data obfuscation or encryption, making it difficult or impossible for investigators to access and interpret digital information.

To illustrate, an attacker might use the GnuPG (GNU Privacy Guard) command-line tool to encrypt sensitive files:

cssCopy code

```
gpg --encrypt --recipient recipient@example.com sensitive_file.txt
```

This command encrypts the "sensitive_file.txt" using the recipient's public key, ensuring that only the recipient with the corresponding private key can decrypt and access the file.

Data destruction, on the other hand, aims to permanently eliminate digital evidence to prevent its recovery by forensic investigators. One common method for data destruction is secure file deletion using utilities like "shred" on Unix-based systems:

bashCopy code

```
shred -u -z -n 5 sensitive_file.txt
```

The "shred" command overwrites the content of the file multiple times with random data before deleting it, making it extremely challenging to recover any meaningful information.

Another anti-forensic technique involves tampering with system logs and event records to remove or modify evidence of malicious activities. Attackers may use command-line tools or scripts to manipulate logs, such as the "auditctl" command on Linux systems:

mathematicaCopy code

```
auditctl -D
```

This command deletes audit rules, effectively suppressing logging of specific events or actions that may be relevant to an investigation.

Furthermore, attackers may employ rootkits and root-level malware to conceal their presence and tamper with system components that provide forensic data. These sophisticated pieces of software can subvert the operating system and interfere with the normal functioning of security tools and logging mechanisms.

To demonstrate, an attacker might use a rootkit to modify the behavior of the "ps" command, which is used to display information about running processes:

Copy code

```
ps
```

The rootkit could intercept the "ps" command and manipulate its output to hide the presence of malicious processes.

Anti-forensic techniques can also extend to network communications. Attackers may use encrypted or anonymized communication channels to obscure their activities. For instance, they might leverage the Tor network for anonymous browsing and communication:

rCopy code

```
tor-browser
```

The Tor browser routes traffic through a network of volunteer-run servers, making it challenging for investigators to trace the origin or destination of network traffic.

To counter anti-forensics and data destruction, forensic investigators employ various methods and tools designed to recover and analyze digital evidence, even in the face of sophisticated evasion techniques.

For data recovery, forensic experts often rely on specialized hardware and software solutions that can restore data from damaged or overwritten storage media. These tools attempt to reconstruct deleted or damaged files, providing valuable insights for investigations.

Additionally, investigators work to establish secure forensic procedures that preserve the integrity and admissibility of digital evidence. This includes creating forensic images of storage devices, maintaining chain-of-custody records, and documenting every step of the investigation to ensure that evidence remains valid in legal proceedings.

To mitigate anti-forensic tactics, organizations must implement robust cybersecurity measures that include continuous monitoring and detection capabilities. Employing endpoint detection and response (EDR) solutions can help identify suspicious or malicious activities that may indicate anti-forensic efforts.

Furthermore, educating employees about the importance of data security and the risks associated with anti-forensics can help prevent insider threats and ensure that personnel understand the consequences of engaging in such activities.

In summary, anti-forensics and data destruction represent a constant challenge for digital forensic investigators and cybersecurity professionals. As attackers become more sophisticated in their techniques, defenders must stay vigilant and adapt their strategies to protect against these threats while preserving the integrity of digital evidence for investigations and legal proceedings.

Evasion techniques in network traffic refer to the methods employed by malicious actors to hide or disguise their activities within data packets and network communications. These techniques are used to evade detection by security systems, such as intrusion detection systems (IDS) and intrusion prevention systems (IPS), which rely on traffic analysis to identify and block suspicious or malicious behavior.

One common evasion technique involves fragmentation of network packets. Attackers can break a single data packet into smaller fragments, making it more challenging for security systems to reassemble and analyze the content. For example, a simple command to fragment a packet using the "ping" utility on a Unix-based system would look like this:

rCopy code

```
ping -s 1500 -c 1 target.example.com
```

In this command, the "-s" flag specifies the packet size, and "-c 1" indicates sending a single packet to the target host. By manipulating the packet size, attackers can create fragmentation that can be difficult to analyze, potentially allowing malicious content to go unnoticed.

Another evasion technique involves the use of protocol anomalies or non-standard behaviors. Attackers can craft network packets that deviate from the expected behavior of legitimate traffic. For instance, some network security systems may expect certain protocols to follow specific standards, and any deviation from these standards can trigger suspicion.

For instance, an attacker might use the "hping3" command-line tool to send packets with non-standard TCP flags:

cssCopy code

```
hping3 -S -F -A -P -U -Y target.example.com
```

In this example, the "-S," "-F," "-A," "-P," "-U," and "-Y" flags represent various TCP flags that can be set in the packets. By sending packets with a combination of flags that do not conform to typical TCP communication, an attacker may attempt to evade detection.

Additionally, attackers can use encoding and obfuscation techniques to hide malicious content within network traffic. This can include encoding data in various formats, such as Base64 or hexadecimal, to make it appear as harmless data.

Decoding the content can be challenging for security systems that do not recognize the encoded format.

For instance, an attacker might encode a malicious script using Base64 and embed it within a legitimate-looking HTTP request: bashCopy code

GET /index.html HTTP/1.1 Host: target.example.com User-Agent: Mozilla/5.0 (Windows NT 10.0; Win64; x64) AppleWebKit/537.36 (KHTML, like Gecko) Chrome/58.0.3029.110 Safari/537.36 Accept: text/html,application/xhtml+xml,application/xml;q=0.9,image/webp,image/apng,*/*;q=0.8 Accept-Encoding: gzip, deflate, br Accept-Language: en-US,en;q=0.9 Connection: close Cookie: session_id=12345 Content-Type: text/plain;charset=UTF-8 eval(atob('aWYgKHNOcnBvcygnZXRhZylpKSB7CiAgcmV0dXJulF RydWU7CnOK'));

The Base64-encoded script within the "eval" function may contain malicious instructions, and security systems may struggle to identify the threat within the seemingly innocuous HTTP request.

Furthermore, evasion techniques can involve leveraging encrypted communications, such as using HTTPS (HTTP Secure) or encrypted tunnels like Virtual Private Networks (VPNs). Encryption encrypts the data transferred between endpoints, making it difficult for network security systems to inspect the content for malicious activity.

To counter evasion techniques in network traffic, organizations deploy advanced network security solutions that can analyze traffic more effectively. These solutions may include next-generation firewalls (NGFWs) with deep packet inspection capabilities, which can decrypt and inspect encrypted traffic.

Additionally, machine learning and behavioral analysis can help identify anomalous network behavior that may indicate evasion attempts. Security teams can use threat intelligence feeds and continuous monitoring to stay informed about emerging evasion tactics and adjust their defenses accordingly.

Moreover, implementing best practices for secure network configurations and regular security updates can help reduce vulnerabilities that attackers may exploit as part of their evasion techniques. It's essential for organizations to maintain a proactive and adaptive approach to network security to stay ahead of evolving threats and evasion tactics.

Chapter 9: Reporting and Communication Skills

Effective reporting of findings is a crucial aspect of any cybersecurity operation, as it serves as the bridge between technical analysis and decision-making by providing actionable insights to stakeholders. In this chapter, we will delve into the importance of clear and concise reporting in the cybersecurity field.

When conducting cybersecurity assessments, whether it's a vulnerability assessment, penetration test, or incident response investigation, the findings and observations need to be communicated effectively to the relevant parties. This communication involves creating detailed reports that not only document the technical aspects of the assessment but also provide context and recommendations for remediation.

A well-structured cybersecurity report should begin with an executive summary that provides a high-level overview of the key findings, risks, and recommended actions. This section is vital for senior management and non-technical stakeholders who may not have the time or expertise to delve into the technical details.

For example, when generating a penetration test report, you might use CLI commands to extract relevant data:

Copy code

```
nmap -sV -oA scan_results target.example.com
```

The "nmap" command conducts a service version scan on the target host and saves the results in various formats, including an XML file that can be included in the report.

Following the executive summary, the report should provide a detailed technical analysis of the vulnerabilities or incidents discovered during the assessment. This includes information about the affected systems, the severity of the issues, and the potential impact on the organization.

To enhance the clarity of the report, consider using data visualization techniques. For instance, you can create graphs or charts to illustrate the distribution of vulnerabilities by severity or their presence across different parts of the network.

When discussing vulnerabilities, it's crucial to provide a clear description of the issue, including its technical details and the methodology used for identification. CLI commands and examples can be invaluable in conveying this information effectively. For instance, when discussing a SQL injection vulnerability, you might include a snippet of the vulnerable code along with the relevant SQL query:

```
sqlCopy code
Vulnerable Code Snippet: ----------------------- ... $sql = "SELECT * FROM users WHERE username = '" . $_POST['username'] . "' AND password = '" . $_POST['password'] . "'"; ... Exploitation Example: ---------------------- Input: ' OR '1'='1 SQL Query: SELECT * FROM users WHERE username = '' OR '1'='1' AND password = '' OR '1'='1' ...
```

Including CLI commands and code snippets can help technical readers understand the issue more clearly and replicate the findings for validation.

Furthermore, it's essential to provide recommendations for remediation or mitigation. These recommendations should be practical and actionable, addressing not only the technical aspects but also the business impact and potential compliance requirements. For example, if a report identifies outdated software as a vulnerability, the remediation recommendation might include instructions for updating the software along with a timeline for completion.

Moreover, the report should prioritize the identified vulnerabilities or incidents based on their severity and potential impact. This prioritization helps organizations allocate resources efficiently and address the most critical issues first.

In addition to providing technical details and recommendations, a well-rounded cybersecurity report should consider the larger context. This may involve discussing the organization's risk tolerance, compliance requirements, and potential legal and reputational implications of the findings.

The language used in the report should strike a balance between technical accuracy and accessibility to non-technical stakeholders. Avoid jargon and overly complex technical terms, but ensure that the report conveys the gravity of the findings accurately.

Additionally, cybersecurity reports should adhere to established templates and standards, which may vary depending on the organization or industry. Following a standardized format ensures consistency in reporting and makes it easier for stakeholders to navigate and understand the information presented.

It's essential to consider the audience when crafting cybersecurity reports. Technical staff may require in-depth technical details and CLI command outputs to replicate findings, while executives and non-technical stakeholders need a high-level overview and a clear understanding of the business impact.

Collaboration between the technical and non-technical teams is crucial in the reporting process. Technical experts can provide valuable insights and recommendations, while non-technical stakeholders can offer perspectives on business priorities and risk tolerance.

Furthermore, cybersecurity reports should be reviewed and validated before finalization. Peer reviews by colleagues or subject matter experts can help identify any inaccuracies or omissions in the report.

Once the report is complete, it should be disseminated to the relevant parties promptly. Timely reporting is essential, especially when addressing critical vulnerabilities or responding to security incidents. Additionally, secure channels should be used to transmit sensitive information to maintain confidentiality.

Finally, after the report is delivered, it's crucial to track the progress of remediation efforts and follow up with stakeholders as needed. Regular updates on the status of remediation actions can help ensure that identified vulnerabilities are addressed effectively.

In summary, effective reporting of findings is a fundamental aspect of cybersecurity operations. Clear and concise reports that provide technical details, recommendations, and context are essential for organizations to understand their security posture and take appropriate actions to mitigate risks. Crafting these reports requires a balance between technical accuracy and accessibility, as well as collaboration between technical and non-technical teams to ensure that cybersecurity assessments lead to meaningful improvements in an organization's security posture.

In the realm of cybersecurity, effective communication with stakeholders and clients is a critical component of a successful cybersecurity program. It bridges the gap between technical experts and decision-makers, ensuring that security measures align with business objectives and risk tolerance.

When communicating with stakeholders and clients, it's essential to adopt a clear and concise approach. Cybersecurity concepts and technical details can be complex, so conveying information in an understandable manner is paramount. Avoid jargon and acronyms that may be unfamiliar to non-technical individuals.

One way to facilitate communication is through the use of plain language summaries and explanations. For instance, when discussing a security incident, explain it in terms of its impact on the organization's operations or data, rather than delving into intricate technical details.

In situations where technical information is necessary, consider using analogies to help non-technical stakeholders grasp complex concepts. For example, likening a firewall to a security checkpoint at an airport can make it easier to understand its role in protecting the network.

Another vital aspect of effective communication is tailoring the message to the audience. Different stakeholders have varying levels of technical expertise and concerns. For example, the CEO may be primarily interested in the overall risk to the business, while the IT department may require detailed technical information.

Furthermore, transparency is key when communicating with stakeholders and clients. It's essential to provide honest and accurate information about the cybersecurity landscape, including any vulnerabilities, incidents, or risks that may impact the organization. Transparency fosters trust and allows stakeholders to make informed decisions.

Moreover, cybersecurity professionals should prioritize active listening when engaging with stakeholders. Actively listening to their concerns, questions, and feedback demonstrates a commitment to understanding their needs and addressing their issues. This two-way communication ensures that cybersecurity efforts align with the organization's goals and priorities.

In the context of a security incident, it's crucial to keep stakeholders informed about the progress of the incident response efforts. Provide regular updates on the incident's status, actions taken to mitigate the impact, and anticipated timelines for resolution. This level of transparency can help manage expectations and alleviate concerns.

When presenting findings or recommendations to stakeholders and clients, it's valuable to highlight the potential business impact. Describe how specific cybersecurity measures or vulnerabilities may affect the organization's operations, reputation, and financial health. This approach enables decision-makers to prioritize actions based on business objectives.

Moreover, when discussing cybersecurity risks and measures, consider providing options and alternatives. Decision-makers may need to choose between various approaches, such as investing in new security technologies, enhancing employee training, or accepting a certain level of risk. Presenting these options allows stakeholders to make informed choices aligned with their risk appetite.

In situations where immediate action is required, it's essential to convey the urgency of the matter. For instance, if a critical vulnerability is identified, emphasize the need for prompt remediation to mitigate potential risks. CLI commands may be used to demonstrate the severity of the issue and its potential exploitation. For instance:

markdownCopy code

Severity Assessment: -------------------- Vulnerability: Apache Struts Remote Code Execution CVE ID: CVE-2017-5638 Impact: High Exploitation Risk: Critical CLI Command to Verify Vulnerability: ----------------------------------- nmap -p 80,443 --script http-vuln-cve2017-5638 <target_ip>

In this example, the CLI command "nmap" is used to assess the target's vulnerability to the Apache Struts Remote Code Execution vulnerability (CVE-2017-5638). The severity and exploitation risk are highlighted to convey the urgency of addressing the issue.

To enhance the effectiveness of communication, consider using visual aids such as charts, graphs, or diagrams. These visuals can simplify complex concepts and provide a quick overview of key points. For instance, a bar chart showing the distribution of cybersecurity risks by category can offer a visual representation of where the organization's greatest vulnerabilities lie.

Additionally, cybersecurity professionals should be prepared to answer questions and address concerns from stakeholders and clients. This requires a deep understanding of the technical aspects of cybersecurity, as well as the ability to translate this knowledge into practical, actionable advice.

In summary, effective communication with stakeholders and clients is essential in the field of cybersecurity. It involves conveying complex technical information in a clear and understandable manner, tailoring messages to the audience, prioritizing transparency, and providing options and recommendations. CLI commands and visuals can be valuable tools in conveying technical details, while active listening and responsiveness to questions and concerns foster trust and collaboration. Ultimately, effective communication enables organizations to make informed decisions that enhance their cybersecurity posture and align with their business objectives.

Chapter 10: Building a Career in Ethical Hacking and Red Teaming

Navigating the vast landscape of cybersecurity education and certifications can be a daunting task, but it's a critical journey for those looking to establish a career in this dynamic field. Whether you're just starting or seeking to advance your knowledge and skills, understanding the available educational and certification paths is essential.

One of the primary considerations when embarking on a cybersecurity journey is determining your current level of expertise and your ultimate career goals. Cybersecurity encompasses a broad spectrum of roles, from entry-level positions to highly specialized experts. Thus, identifying your specific interests and aspirations will help you choose the right path.

For those new to cybersecurity, a foundational understanding of information technology (IT) is often the first step. IT fundamentals provide the groundwork upon which cybersecurity knowledge is built. You can explore this area through courses offered by institutions, online tutorials, or even by obtaining a basic IT certification, such as CompTIA IT Fundamentals (ITF+).

As you progress, gaining a solid understanding of networking is crucial. Many cyber threats and attacks target network vulnerabilities, making networking knowledge essential for cybersecurity professionals. Certifications like CompTIA Network+ or Cisco Certified Network Associate (CCNA) can be beneficial at this stage.

Once you've established a strong IT and networking foundation, you can delve into more specialized areas of cybersecurity. The Certified Information Systems Security Professional (CISSP) certification is a widely recognized credential for professionals with expertise in various aspects of cybersecurity, including risk management, security architecture, and access control.

If you have a specific interest in ethical hacking and penetration testing, the Certified Ethical Hacker (CEH) certification is designed to validate your skills in assessing and securing computer systems. This certification involves hands-on training in identifying vulnerabilities and exploiting them within legal and ethical boundaries.

For those aiming to specialize further, certifications like the Certified Information Security Manager (CISM) and Certified Information Systems Auditor (CISA) are ideal choices. CISM focuses on information risk management and governance, while CISA emphasizes information system auditing and control.

Moreover, if your career path involves safeguarding cloud environments, you can explore cloud-specific certifications like the Amazon Web Services (AWS) Certified Security - Specialty or the Certified Cloud Security Professional (CCSP) offered by (ISC)².

In addition to these certification paths, many universities and colleges offer bachelor's and master's degree programs in cybersecurity or related fields, such as information assurance. These programs provide in-depth knowledge and often include hands-on lab experiences, research opportunities, and internship placements.

Furthermore, online learning platforms have become valuable resources for cybersecurity education. Platforms like Coursera, edX, and Udacity offer a wide range of cybersecurity courses and even specialized online degrees. These platforms provide flexibility, allowing individuals to study at their own pace while gaining valuable knowledge and skills.

Hands-on experience is a crucial aspect of a cybersecurity education. Creating a virtual lab environment using tools like VirtualBox, VMware, or cloud-based services can provide a safe space for practicing various cybersecurity techniques and exercises. This hands-on practice is essential for applying theoretical knowledge in real-world scenarios.

Open-source cybersecurity tools and resources are readily available for individuals seeking to sharpen their skills. Tools like Wireshark for network analysis, Metasploit for penetration testing, and Snort for intrusion detection can be invaluable for hands-on practice. Exploring these tools in a controlled environment helps develop practical skills.

Engaging with the cybersecurity community is another vital aspect of your educational journey. Joining forums, attending conferences, participating in Capture The Flag (CTF) challenges, and collaborating with peers can enhance your knowledge and provide networking opportunities. Many cybersecurity professionals actively share their insights and experiences, which can be highly beneficial.

Ultimately, the educational and certification paths in cybersecurity are diverse and adaptable to individual goals and interests. Continual learning and staying updated with the evolving threat landscape are essential aspects of a successful career in cybersecurity. Whether you choose to pursue certifications, degrees, or a combination of both, the key is to remain dedicated, curious, and committed to safeguarding the digital world.

Navigating the job market in cybersecurity requires a strategic approach and a deep understanding of the industry's dynamics. As the digital landscape continues to evolve, the demand for skilled cybersecurity professionals is on the rise. However, it's essential to recognize that this field is not a one-size-fits-all, and various roles exist within the cybersecurity ecosystem.

First and foremost, it's crucial to identify your specific career goals within cybersecurity. This will determine the skills and certifications you need to acquire. Some common career paths in cybersecurity include security analyst, ethical hacker, penetration tester, security consultant, and security architect, among others. Each role has its unique responsibilities and required expertise.

Once you have a clear career goal in mind, it's time to assess your current skillset and qualifications. If you're new to the field, starting with entry-level positions such as a security analyst or junior penetration tester is advisable. These roles often require foundational knowledge in IT and cybersecurity, which can be acquired through certifications like CompTIA Security+ or Certified Information Systems Security Professional (CISSP) Associate.

For those with some experience or relevant educational backgrounds, mid-level positions like security engineer or ethical hacker may be attainable. These roles typically require more specialized knowledge and skills, which can be acquired through certifications such as Certified Ethical Hacker (CEH) or Certified Information Security Manager (CISM).

To move into senior or leadership roles within cybersecurity, extensive experience and expertise are essential. Chief Information Security Officer (CISO), security director, and security consultant positions require a deep understanding of cybersecurity strategy, risk management, and governance. Certifications like Certified Information Systems Security Professional (CISSP), Certified Information Security Manager (CISM), or Certified Information Systems Auditor (CISA) are highly regarded in these positions.

Networking plays a crucial role in finding job opportunities in cybersecurity. Joining professional organizations like (ISC)², ISACA, or local cybersecurity meetups can provide valuable connections and job leads. Additionally, online platforms like LinkedIn can help you connect with professionals in the field and explore job openings.

When applying for cybersecurity positions, tailoring your resume and cover letter to the specific role is vital. Highlight relevant skills, certifications, and experiences that align with the job requirements. Emphasize any hands-on experience or practical knowledge gained through labs, personal projects, or Capture The Flag (CTF) challenges.

Interview preparation is equally important. Be ready to discuss your technical skills, problem-solving abilities, and knowledge of cybersecurity concepts. Potential employers may also assess your ability to handle real-world scenarios, so be prepared to explain how you would respond to security incidents or breaches.

Incorporating hands-on experience into your cybersecurity journey is highly beneficial. Setting up a home lab environment using virtualization software like VirtualBox or VMware allows you to practice cybersecurity techniques and gain practical skills. Engaging in Capture The Flag (CTF) challenges on platforms like Hack The Box or TryHackMe can further enhance your problem-solving abilities.

Building a portfolio of your work is another effective way to demonstrate your skills to potential employers. Document your progress on personal projects, challenges, or security assessments. This can include write-ups detailing your approach and solutions to various cybersecurity tasks. Sharing this portfolio on platforms like GitHub or a personal blog can showcase your abilities to hiring managers.

Networking and learning should be ongoing processes in your cybersecurity career. Stay up-to-date with industry trends, emerging threats, and evolving technologies. Subscribing to cybersecurity news sources, following blogs and podcasts, and attending conferences can help you stay informed and connected within the field.

One of the unique aspects of the cybersecurity job market is the constant demand for skilled professionals. Cyber threats are continually evolving, creating a continuous need for experts who can protect organizations' digital assets. This demand offers excellent job security and opportunities for career advancement.

In summary, navigating the job market in cybersecurity involves defining your career goals, acquiring the necessary skills and certifications, networking with professionals, tailoring your application materials, and continually enhancing your skills through hands-on practice and learning. With dedication and a strategic approach, you can embark on a fulfilling and rewarding career in the ever-expanding world of cybersecurity.

Conclusion

In the world of cybersecurity, the battle against cyber threats rages on, and the Trojan horse remains one of the most insidious and persistent adversaries. As we conclude our journey through the pages of "Trojan Exposed," a comprehensive book bundle dedicated to tackling this formidable foe, we are armed not only with knowledge but with the tools and strategies needed to defend against and ultimately eradicate this type of malware.

In Book 1, "Trojan Exposed: A Beginner's Guide to Cybersecurity," we laid the foundation for understanding the world of cybersecurity and the threat landscape that surrounds us. We explored the basics of Trojans, their history, and the fundamental principles of cybersecurity. This book served as a critical starting point for readers, whether they were new to the field or seeking to reinforce their cybersecurity fundamentals.

Book 2, "Trojan Exposed: Mastering Advanced Threat Detection," took our journey a step further. Here, we delved deep into the intricacies of Trojan variants and advanced detection techniques. We equipped readers with the knowledge and expertise to identify and combat sophisticated Trojan threats. By mastering these advanced detection methods, we strengthened our cybersecurity defenses and fortified our organizations against evolving cyber threats.

In Book 3, "Trojan Exposed: Expert Strategies for Cyber Resilience," we shifted our focus to resilience and preparedness. Recognizing that cybersecurity is not solely about defense but also about recovery, we explored strategies for building cyber resilience. By implementing these expert strategies, readers gained the ability to withstand and recover from cyberattacks, ensuring the continuity of their operations.

Finally, in Book 4, "Trojan Exposed: Red Team Tactics and Ethical Hacking," we embraced the offensive side of cybersecurity. We learned about the techniques employed by ethical hackers and red teamers to simulate real-world cyberattacks. By understanding the adversary's perspective and adopting proactive measures, readers were better equipped to protect their systems, identify vulnerabilities, and enhance their overall cybersecurity posture.

As we reflect on our journey through "Trojan Exposed," we recognize that the fight against cyber threats, particularly Trojans, is an ongoing battle. Cybercriminals are persistent and continuously adapt their tactics, making it crucial for us to remain vigilant and informed. However, armed with the knowledge and insights gained from these four books, readers are better equipped to face the evolving challenges of cybersecurity.

In closing, we would like to emphasize the importance of a holistic approach to cybersecurity. While each book in this bundle focuses on specific aspects of Trojan threats and cybersecurity, they are all interconnected. The beginner's guide, advanced threat detection, expert strategies for resilience, and red team tactics all contribute to a comprehensive cybersecurity strategy.

We hope that the knowledge and skills acquired from "Trojan Exposed" empower you to protect your systems, networks, and data. Cybersecurity is not a one-time endeavor but an ongoing commitment to safeguarding our digital world. With dedication, continuous learning, and the right tools, we can collectively strengthen our cyber defenses and mitigate the ever-present threat of Trojans and other malicious actors.

Thank you for embarking on this journey with us, and may your cybersecurity efforts be resilient and successful in the face of evolving challenges.